Praise for A Heart Traced in Sand

"A touching testimony to the power of a father's love for his daughter. Sensitively written, poignant, and inspiring."

Jack Heinowitz, PhD
Author of *Pregnant Fathers*
and *Fathering Right from the Start*

"Naomi's short life is an inspiration to all of us. She lived fully and left behind an indelible trail that will fill the heart and soul of any person who steps on it."

Malidoma Somé
Author of *The Healing Wisdom of Africa*
and *Of Water and the Spirit*

D1471020

A Heart Traced in Sand

A Heart Traced in Sand

Reflections on a Daughter's Struggle for Life

Steven Boone

TWIN-FLAMES

Santa Fe, New Mexico

Twin-Flames Publishing
PO Box 23503
Santa Fe, NM 87502

Editors: Ellen Kleiner, Ann Mason
Cover design: Steven Boone
Back cover photo: Jill Martin

A Heart Traced in Sand is factually true except that some names have been altered to protect the privacy of individuals.

Publisher's Cataloging-in-Publication Data

Boone, Steven, 1952-
A heart traced in sand : reflections on a daughter's struggle for life/
Steven Boone. -- 1st ed.
p. cm.
Includes bibliographical references.
LCCN: 00-193266
ISBN: 0 9706046-0-2

    1. Boone, Naomi.   2. Ewing's sarcoma--Patients--New Mexico--
Biography.   3. Ewing's sarcoma--Patients--Family relationships.
4. Tumors in children--Patients--New Mexico--Biography.
5. Cancer--Religious aspects.
1. Title.

    RC280.B6B66 2001   362.1'989299471'0092
                                QB101-200120

10 9 8 7 6 5 4 3 2 1

That the pure light may banish the darkness of despair

In appreciation . . .

I am particularly grateful to the many, many people who stood firmly by Naomi during her struggle. I regret that space does not permit mention of everyone's name, but I feel I must especially acknowledge my wife Jean. Also, our daughter Sarah; Naomi's mother Kathleen; my physician cousins David and Ben Boone, and the doctors and staff in Dallas, Texas; my mother and father, Richard and Chloris Boone; Jean's parents, Charles and Mary Tobias; Naomi's teacher and friend, Barbara Miller; teen chums Alexis Diaz and Adella Garcia; Gary Myers; the "healing team" in Santa Barbara, California; Jill Martin, who took priceless photographs; Ann, Ben, Ben Jr., Emma, and Carrie Brode, who gave Naomi a home away from home; my brother Brent and his family, with whom she also lived; Andrei, "the Russian healer" Peggy Myers, who gave her time and talent to help edit; and the many people who were with Naomi in spirit, and prayed.

The poem appearing on pages 204–205, from *A Splintered Mirror: Chinese Poetry from the Democracy Movement*, is reprinted by permission of North Point Press, a division of Farrar, Straus and Giroux, LLC. Translation copyright © 1991 by Donald Finkel.

CONTENTS

*"The same wind that uproots the trees,
makes the grasses shine."*
Rumi

PREFACE

When this book began, it was meant to be an exclamation of joy at the miracles that happen in life when we have faith. I wished to share the glad tidings of "spirit over matter," which I had witnessed firsthand. That was when my eighteen-year-old daughter, Naomi, seemed to be winning her long-shot battle against Ewing's sarcoma, a rare cancer that had been diagnosed in its late stages, already having metastasized into her lungs from her hip. At the time, we believed prayer and faith would provide us the extra power needed to beat Naomi's poor odds and claim an astounding victory. But our confidence was dealt a devastating blow, for it was discovered that although Naomi's cancer had been knocked down, it still had strength, and to our terrible dismay, it came back. Eventually it took her life, and at the same time completely tested my faith and beliefs, leaving a different picture than I had envisioned as the subject of this book.

When the tide turned against Naomi and it became clear that the triumph we had prayed for might not occur, a grand picture of the human soul remained, portraying even more vividly spirit's victory over matter. For the pain and loss Naomi was experiencing did not destroy her love of life; rather, they enhanced it. Even during gruesome chemotherapy treatments, she wrote in her diary: "Life is so beautiful, I cherish it and want to be able to see every part of it."

So profound was her depth of feeling for life, that just two days before her death she said to a friend, "I love my body, it has been so good to me." Only by Naomi's connectedness to eternal God could her soul soar above her painful last moments, enabling her to look tenderly at her stricken body and with some of her last breaths say, "I love you."

The further I went in writing this book, the more I realized that God had heard our every prayer and had watched over each moment of our struggle, as is evident in the remarkable occurrences that appear in these chapters. The description of events follows the orientation of my own soul, yet is open to any number of inspirational interpretations. In addition to these experiences, you will read about my struggle to make sense of the mystery of life while learning how hardships help define us. Finally, a mystical dialogue about faith ensues, drawing from the fertile fields of dreams, the writings of holy texts, and my perceptions of the spiritual aspect of Naomi in her struggle.

Each chapter begins with a quotation from Naomi. It is a privilege to share intimately Naomi's experiences as well as her writings that they may serve as inspiration to others.

SPIRIT UNFOLDING

*I know I am surrounded by spirits, and that is the feeling
of the Lord.*

As a heart traced in sand upon the shore vanishes under the onrushing waves of a fathomless ocean, the hand of God swept over my precious nineteen-year-old daughter Naomi, and she disappeared, leaving me with only memories. Although we had been linked tightly by bonds of flesh and spirit, the flesh was now broken but the tie between our spirits remained.

When I arrived at her side, Naomi was still in her bed, where she had died an hour earlier, wearing a red and blue T-shirt and khaki shorts. The oxygen equipment attached to her face for the last week was gone, and gazing at her through my tears, I sought to understand an expression I had never before seen on her face. The signs of her terrible two-year struggle with cancer were lifted, and it was as if I were beholding a person who had just drowned in an ocean of light. Although the vestiges of youth were still in her face, I also glimpsed an ancient knowledge in her, as if she had finally discovered a lofty secret she had been longing to know. At the corners of her closed eyes, she seemed to be smiling.

Although unaware of it at the time, I now realize God had prepared me for a catastrophe years before in a dream that has haunted and mystified me ever since. While on vacation at a resort in Bend, Oregon, I awoke one morning and tried to understand the astonishing occurrences of my sleep, rehearsing this dream:

It was just getting dark one late autumn evening, and the last light seemed to hang in the air. I was alone, lying on my back on a short platform in an open clearing in the woods. Looking up at the sky through the bare limbs of trees, I suddenly saw a hawk fly by. Then I heard the roar of wings beating the air, and abruptly from my right, just above the treetops, a great flock of birds passed swiftly in front of me and disappeared to my left. My spirit and senses were completely awakened by this fabulous orchestration of nature, and I found myself praying, "Oh, God, give me a sign!" That instant, as if in response to my plea, in the darkening sky I saw an incandescent shooting star. I was now at rapt attention.

Next, I was aware of a man riding on a horse close to where I lay. His dog came over and licked my hand in a friendly way. Then I heard the beat of horses' hoofs, and in the next instant the rider on horseback appeared before me—an Indian warrior in superb condition and wearing only a leather breechcloth. He was bareback upon a mighty chestnut-red stallion that was fully alert to his every command. There was nothing tenuous about horse and rider; they were all purpose and power. Reaching back in one steady motion, the warrior drew an arrow from his quiver, placed it in his bow, effortlessly drew back his bowstring, and released it. At that moment, I realized I was not alone on the platform, for lying next to me was a young boy. In a split second, the arrow whizzed by me and struck the child's heart!

I thought of escaping . . . Then I awoke with a gasp, feeling startled and deeply hurt.

Numerous times I pondered this dream, even going over it in psychoanalysis. It seemed a vision of beauty and power, but what puzzled me was the warrior's arrow sent into the child's open and defenseless heart. I began to think it was perhaps a sign for my childhood to end and my adult warrior self to emerge. To help myself understand the powerful symbolic imagery, I made a large painting of a warrior holding an arrow in a drawn bowstring. Not until Naomi was suddenly diagnosed with advanced cancer did I gradually comprehend that the dream might have signified future events in not only my life but also my child's. Fortunately, I did not witness dying. Maybe, I thought, the dream did not foretell death but rather the transfer of power.

When I first met the woman who would be Naomi's mother, we exchanged greetings on a winter morning at the mailbox in front of the downtown Santa Fe Post Office. I could not have guessed then what she would mean to me—that from the two of us, Naomi would come into the world and forever our souls would be linked. My soul was almost intuitively drawn to this woman. We engaged easily, and I liked her openness and easy laughter as she stood in front of me wearing a yellow ski jacket, her auburn hair tucked into a red knit cap. Something else drew me to her as well, which at the time I hardly understood. My soul glimpsed a maiden standing on an uneven precipice, in danger of falling, and instinctively I reached out to hold her, perhaps because I too have an ambient personality, and had at times in my life stood perilously on a precipice.

Kathleen spoke fluent Spanish, which she had learned while growing up in the Canal Zone of Panama, and now at the age of thirty was unemployed. I was twenty-seven and a budding artist, fresh out of art college. My artistic soul was attracted to her because she had an enigmatic, childlike presence and seemed full of contradictions: she was fragile and stubborn, hopeful and lost, friendly yet distant. And there was always that awesome precipice she stood upon.

After we married and she became pregnant, Kathleen began rising at dawn to light a candle and call angels to visit the being growing inside of her. I prayed for our unborn child, dedicating it to God, asking that it be made praiseworthy and grow and develop under divine guidance.

We chose to have a home birth attended by a local doctor who worked in tandem with a midwife. Then we thought about naming our child; for a boy we agreed on Jason, and for a girl, Naomi, because I liked the strong vowels strung together. In my heart I felt slightly more yearning for a daughter than a son, but looked happily toward the arrival of either. Considering the pregnancy a period of spiritual attainment, Kathleen and I both joyfully anticipated the birth.

Around 4:30 on the morning of January 11, 1980, I woke up to see Kathleen sitting on the edge of our bed. "Steven," she said, "I'm having contractions. I think the baby is coming. Please call the midwife." I called, and she arrived at 5:00 A.M., followed two hours later by the doctor. By then, soothing music was coming from the record player, and as I held Kathleen's hand, she groaned in exertion. After six hours of labor, our baby emerged and gave a little cry.

The midwife clamped the umbilical cord, and I cut it. Then the doctor pronounced Naomi a healthy child. Looking at her remarkable little red body, I was elated. Kathleen, exhausted, smiled and put her to her breast to nurse.

From the start, Naomi was a constant source of wonder and delight to us. We all slept in the same bed the first year. As a toddler, she was an easy child, robust and healthy, with straight blonde hair, and when she turned three, I bought her a little easel and crayons, and was surprised how eagerly she drew. Gripping a crayon tightly in her little fist, she expressed herself confidently,

Naomi, age two, making art

sometimes covering entire sheets of paper with colorful marks from top to bottom and side to side. Soon, recognizable forms emerged—smiling figures with outstretched stick arms arose from the ground, sometimes with a radiant sun above them. Other times, a small figure appeared inside a larger one; both smiling. Flowers grew up from green earth toward the stretching rays of the sun. Hearts were everywhere, even on balloons drifting up in the air. She once drew a house in a field with raindrops falling from the sky, smoke coming from the chimney, and people in all the windows. Her fits of creativity came in short, fervent, fluid bursts of unconstrained freedom, while I spent more protracted hours trying to master my expressions. Sometimes we worked side by side, both at our easels, and at other times she sat on my lap as I painted. Eventually, unable to support the family as an artist, I took a job as a waiter, and also established a landscaping business. Whenever I could, I returned to my artwork.

Even now, I don't entirely understand the terrible circumstances that befell our marriage. When Naomi was two and a half years old, shortly after being weaned, Kathleen began suffering from food allergies, and we started arguing. As emotions heated up, exacerbated by youth and poverty, I was surprised to learn that Kathleen had previously suffered from mental illness. The Bahá'í religion, to which I have belonged since age twenty, discourages divorce, instead advocating patience, reconciliation, and harmony. After a year of turmoil in the household, however, when Kathleen said she wanted a divorce, I decided not to oppose her wish.

Although only three and a half years old, Naomi sensed something was wrong when I moved out of the house and she began spending time with Kathleen and me separately. During the divorce and thereafter, Kathleen's mental condition steadily deteriorated. She was suspicious of individuals close to her, talked to herself and to imaginary people, and complained of hidden bombs and intricate conspiracies targeting her. It was painful to see her coming apart, especially in front of Naomi, now four years old. Since the court had granted me full custody, Naomi remained under my care, but still spent time with her mother until Kathleen was sent to a mental hospital. I took solace in the thought that Naomi was protected somewhat by her innocence and her inability to understand the tragic aspect of her mother's illness.

As time passed, Naomi's relationship with her mother became a delicate matter, especially since Kathleen exhibited unpredictable behaviors and returned intermittently to the state mental institution. I taught Naomi to look on her with compassion and to remember how loving she had been before becoming ill. Even so, their relationship never regained its earlier peacefulness.

I began taking Naomi to a psychologist twice a week. Chama Ruiz was in her mid-thirties, with short, dark hair and olive skin. The centerpiece of her office was a shallow box filled with sand, and a shelf nearby held small items such as play figures, miniature dolls, knickknacks, and tiny tools. Naomi spent her time on the floor arranging scenes in the sand from objects she picked off the shelf, while Chama watched and sometimes engaged her in conversation about what she was doing. One day when I arrived at the end of a session, Chama showed me Naomi's sand scene and said, "This is very powerful." Two small mirrors stood facing each other in the sand, with a play figure of a child between them. The light reflecting back and forth off the mirrors flashed brilliantly, creating an endless field of light around the little toy figure set in the middle. Indeed, for its simplicity and boldness alone, it seemed a masterful display for a four year old.

Then it came time to find a kindergarten for Naomi. While visiting the local Waldorf school, I met Naomi's future teacher and my future wife, Jean Tobias, a dark-haired, green-eyed woman with a heartwarming smile. Standing alone, dressed simply in a yellow cotton blouse and blue cotton skirt, she seemed poised and eager to greet us. It was love at first sight for me as my pulse quickened and I wanted to know this quiet, refined woman better. Soon my fondness for Jean grew stronger, and after we began dating, when I dropped Naomi off at kindergarten in the morning and saw her, I would slip a love poem into her hand before leaving. The Bahá'í Faith discourages casual intimate relationships, instead endorsing committed unions that lead to strong families, and I knew I wanted to remarry.

Months later, when I was thirty-three years old and Jean was thirty-six, I asked her to marry me and she accepted. So in August 1985, Naomi had a mother figure again whom she could look up to. Jean did important little things with her, such as playing make-believe and rubbing her back while singing to her at bedtime. I, meanwhile, continued operating my landscaping business, now with ten employees, while Jean taught and eventually started her own kindergarten. Although I enjoyed landscaping, I felt as though some part of me was waiting to come to expression in the world, and knew that eventually I would have to honor myself completely by allowing my talent to unfold. In the meantime, I prayed it would not be lost.

In November 1986, our daughter Sarah was born, after which Jean quit teaching to stay at home. About the same time, I realized my dream. With Jean's support, I sold my landscaping business and became a full-time artist, retailing my oil paintings out of an art-district studio. Initially, I worked at my still lifes and landscapes in the back of the studio, displaying the framed paintings on partition walls up front. The next year, we bought six acres of land on the outskirts of Santa Fe, and built a home there with open views of three mountain ranges. Also, I opened a larger gallery, hired salespeople, and showed other artists' work along with my own.

Naomi continued at the Waldorf school which, by its sensitivity to the cycles of nature and the stages of maturity in the children's souls, steadily encouraged her creative temperament. By sixth grade, she was bringing home scores of drawings and watercolor paintings, including abstract exercises involving primary colors, and simpler studies in only two colors. At Halloween, she covered a sheet of white paper with yellow paint and, while it was still wet, used her brush dipped in red to create a smiling orange pumpkin face with orange rays of happiness extending outward over the edges. At home, she used crayons, often drawing interior scenes, such as a princess in a long dress standing at a mirror in her room, with paintings adorning the walls and a table with flowers nearby. She readily let her imagination flow in her art and loved including the details that represent the personality of our lives. It was as if the purity of her soul flowed easily into the world this way.

According to custom at the Waldorf school, the senior eighth grade students begin the year by presenting roses to each child entering the first grade. The event, called the rose ceremony, is held outdoors with parents present. The year that Sarah began first grade, Naomi, in the eighth grade, handed her a rose. It could not have been arranged any better, I thought.

Waldorf education differs from that of the public schools in other ways as well, not the least of which is that year after year, teachers remain with their class. From the second to the eighth grade, Naomi's teacher was Barbara Miller, a lively, middle-aged woman with a friendly disposition. Over the years, Mrs. Miller had become quite familiar with Naomi, understanding her strengths and weaknesses, as well as her family background. When finally she penned her last teacher evaluation at the time of Naomi's graduation from the school, she wrote:

> *What a journey Naomi and Mrs. Miller have been on for the last seven years! I think Naomi is well on her way in life; she is ready for some interesting and exciting changes.*
>
> *Naomi is a courageous, talented, and adventurous young lady. She is fearless in some areas of her life and can win almost anyone's heart. She has a sense of safety and trust in life; and yet, she has had some incredible challenges at a young age. Naomi is ready for expanding, developing, and expressing herself in new ways.*

Naomi had certainly proved her readiness to accept challenges. By the end of eighth grade she was an advanced skier, accustomed to the expert slopes. Also, she had come to love reading, and read avidly at a mature level. She did not seem to care much for fashion or flirting with boys but loved children, which made her the favorite babysitter among our neighbors.

Perhaps her greatest challenge was her relationship with her mother, who at this point had been in and out of the state mental institution for years. When Kathleen was not in the hospital, she lived in an apartment in Santa Fe, where often she was extremely disconcerted and barely able to function. Nonetheless, she demanded to see Naomi at least once a week, and called her frequently. Over time, a pattern began to emerge after Naomi's Sunday afternoon visits with her mother: the following Monday she would fall ill.

I worried about the effect Kathleen's illness was having on Naomi. At times I thought it might be her fate to take on her mother's unbalanced state. Then again, I felt that she must face what life dealt her, and that with sufficient inner strength she could forge her own way in her relationship with her mom. Anytime I noticed that

Naomi did not have a sufficient ego barrier to protect herself from the turbulence in Kathleen's mind, I stayed with them.

What mattered most to me was stated clearly in the Bahá'í writings where Bahá'u'lláh said:

> *O Son of Spirit!*
> *My first counsel is this: Possess a pure, kindly and radiant heart, that thine may be a sovereignty ancient, imperishable and everlasting.* [1]

At that time, who could have known how, in a few short years, Naomi would have to use the courage and fearlessness Mrs. Miller spoke of to face a challenge so fierce that she would lose her sense of safety and trust in life, but then find an inner strength to express her love in ways that would indeed win the hearts of everyone who knew her.

TWISTED FATE

Life is so beautiful. I cherish it and want to be able to see every part of it.

When Naomi began high school, she loved the excitement of joining a big institution with over 500 freshman. Immediately she joined the cross-country team and the German club, later adding track and field, and the ski club to her extracurricular activities. With her long, beautiful legs she especially loved running alongside her teammates to build stamina and strength. Never failing to show up for daily practice, she looked forward to weekend track meets. Her devotion to her coach and teammates continued to grow, and at the state cross-country meet that year, she placed ninth out of more than one hundred competitors.

Committed to advancing her creative abilities, Naomi transferred into an art class taught by Gary Myers, whose excitement about art extended beyond the classroom walls. Mr. Myers often mentored talented youngsters, personally encouraging them to pursue their creative goals. The friendship that began between student and teacher would deepen and last beyond Naomi's graduation.

Naomi, age fifteen, an avid track and field runner

By the second semester of her sophomore year, Naomi was driving to school in an old Toyota Jean had given her. In art classes, as part of her exercises, she used oil paints to copy old master prints onto canvas. On weekends she often helped at my gallery, and seemed to love selecting the placement of objects for exhibition. Fascinated by interior design, she thought of pursuing a career in it.

Santa Fe is packed with art galleries, and often artists' shows of new work in various galleries begin with a public reception known as an "opening." Naomi frequently accompanied me to openings, where we admired art together and mingled with the art community.

Socially, it seemed the only crowd of kids she hung out with was the track team—the focus of her school activities. Her old Waldorf friends had drifted apart, and the only one she maintained regular contact with was Alex Diaz, a quiet youngster from Puerto Rico, who was now being home schooled. The two met regularly and enjoyed weekend sleep-overs.

Then in the summer something happened that would portend the turbulent events to come. On a gray, rainy day, while making a sharp right turn on a winding road leading out of our neighborhood, Naomi was hit head-on by a pickup truck coming from the opposite direction. The impact severely damaged the front of her Toyota, but fortunately, despite being shaken, she was not badly injured. Since her car was still operable, the man who hit her offered to follow her home. Halfway there, however, she was hit head-on by *another* vehicle. Arriving home in tears, she called a neighbor and then the police, who showed up to write a report. By coincidence, I was driving by while Naomi and Jean were with the officer at the accident site. The officer suggested that Naomi be checked by a doctor, especially for insurance purposes. So although she was not complaining of any noticeable injuries, I took her to a local chiropractor. After examining her, he concluded that she had sustained injuries, and she began a series of biweekly remedial treatments.

At the beginning of Naomi's junior year of high school, her passion for team sports was as strong as ever. On weekends when her track meets were at home, our family went to cheer for her. But now, although she exerted all her effort, she only managed to stay in the middle of the pack of runners. At one point, her coach mentioned that she ran with a slight limp, and suggested different running shoes. Naomi herself complained of some pain when she ran, but was so devoted to track that she ignored it. Meanwhile, her doctor continued the treatments and monitored her progress.

That winter Naomi went on a ski trip to Breckenridge, Colorado, with the high school Ski Club. When she returned, I noticed that although she had had a good time, something seemed wrong. Then one evening she coughed, and it caused such pain in her left leg that she could not move. I had to carry her to the car and drive to her doctor's office, where we transported her from the parking lot into the examining room. Taking a look at her, the doctor thought she might have a slight spinal problem that had been exasperated by the coughing. The next day she felt better and returned to school.

For weeks I would sometimes awake at night feeling troubled about Naomi, as if she were contending with an ominous pressure. But my feelings were hard to understand and remained vague, so I would shake them off and drift back to sleep.

As it turned out, the pain in Naomi's leg persisted, and although she pushed herself to move forward, by spring running was too difficult. A routine visit to her gynecologist revealed a hard area on her abdomen. But because she was about to leave with the German Club on a much anticipated two-week trip to Germany, we decided to follow up with another exam upon her return in mid-April.

Naomi called twice from Germany and sent several postcards. Enjoying the adventure greatly, she was proving to be a hardy traveler—one of only a few students who did not get sick from the cold, damp spring weather. Carrying her sketchbook around with her, she made drawings of the German landscape and her immediate surroundings. Her excitement was evident during our drive home from the airport as she talked nonstop about her impressions of the train rides, the green countryside and old churches, and nights out on the town. Opening a little tin container, she said, "Try one of these German cookies, Dad. They're really good!"

In mid-April, the gynecologist, noticing that the hard mass on Naomi's abdomen had increased in size, recommended a CAT scan. By this time Naomi was experiencing great difficulty with her leg, having to lift it into the car with her hands because raising it was so painful. But she did not speak of her distress.

I accompanied Naomi to the local hospital, and sat in a waiting room while she was scanned. The next day, May 5, 1997, we were summoned to a nearby doctor's office for a consultation. I was stunned to find that we were in a cancer clinic. A nurse escorted us into an examining room, where we waited anxiously until a doctor appeared carrying a report. After a moment, he looked grimly at Naomi and told her that according to preliminary findings, it appeared that she had Ewing's sarcoma, an aggressive bone cancer that afflicts children and teenagers. Holding out his hands to profile a ball as big as a grapefruit, and appearing distressed, he said, "The tumor in the hip is very large. Also, it is likely that cancer is in the lungs. Typically, this type of cancer spreads to the lungs and also the brain." Then he ordered a biopsy and brain scan, advising us that Naomi should begin chemotherapy immediately.

The diagnosis seemed unreal. My mind could not fathom that this was really happening because outwardly at least, everything appeared as it always had. But now a terrible equation had been thrust into our lives, causing my mind to shut down and my heart to feel as if a huge weight had been cast upon it. Finally, I mustered the courage to ask the doctor if anyone had survived such a condition, and he replied, yes, it was possible. When Naomi asked if she would be able to run again, the doctor answered, no, he did not think so, causing her to cry. Then clarifying his prognosis, he added that for now she would not be able to run.

Leaving the doctor's office, I had the same feeling in my stomach and pain in my heart that I had experienced years earlier waking up from the dream in which the arrow whizzed by me into the child's heart. Only this time I felt like an arrow of sorrow had been shot into my heart as well. We drove home in stunned silence, each trying to make sense of the tragedy. My soul struggled in twilight, as though a death sentence had just been read to us, yet my ears could not accept it. Naomi, however, showed enormous strength in coping with the news and its implications. On the way home, she told me to keep my chin up and take deep breaths. Searching for words to break the oppression I felt, I assured her that if even one person had survived a situation like hers, then she would also.

A moment later as I was lost in my thoughts, Naomi noticed a young man walking by the road and said, "I know him! That's Brandon from the track team. Let's give him a ride." I pulled over and Brandon hopped into the car. We talked about track meets for a while, until an uneasy silence fell over us. Then Naomi spoke up, saying we had just learned that she had cancer. Little more was said before we dropped Brandon off at home and Naomi wished him luck at the meet that weekend. I too wished him luck, and added sadly, "Naomi is now in a bigger race than running track."

When we arrived home and I shared the news with the family, Naomi said in an emotionally charged voice, "I have to be strong!"

For some time we all stood holding one another and crying, then Jean said, "You *are* strong Naomi, and you can beat this!"

Sarah, ten years old, was bewildered and later asked, "What is cancer?"

The next day, after speaking privately with her English instructor, Naomi announced to the class that she had cancer. According to one of her classmates: "She walked calmly to the front of the class, cleared her throat, and said, 'Maybe some of you have been wondering why I have been missing school and why I haven't been going to track practice. Well, I have been to a specialist about a tumor that was discovered in my hip.' The class was dead quiet. 'I have a serious condition that is pretty advanced, and I'll need to be out of school for a while. I might not even graduate with you guys.' Naomi looked to the floor, and when she glanced up at the class, began to cry, adding, 'Sometimes, people die with my condition.' She sniffed a little and then, smiling through her tears, said, 'But I'll be back.'" The student remarked that this experience was burned forever into her memory.

After school that day, Naomi made a colored-pencil drawing of a woman standing alone in an embroidered blue cloak, with eyes closed, hair radiating outward in twisted rivulets, and a halo encircling her head. By her left shoulder stood a small angel-like figure. From the bottom of the portrait, a thin green reed with tiny leaves grew up in front of the cloaked figure, following a serpentine path all the way out the top of the picture. Then Naomi wrote: "Why am I so afraid of the thing called cancer? I know that a lot of people have gotten through it okay, so why am I so frightened? Is it because of my two grandparents who died of cancer? I know that my family is really concerned. The best thing I can do is be strong and not let it get me down."

The following weekend Naomi again divulged her circumstances with fortitude and grace, this time to the mother of two girls she babysat for on a regular basis. In this woman's words:

I first learned of Naomi's illness on Mother's Day weekend. Naomi, who had been playing "mother" to my two daughters for several years, had left a message on my telephone answering machine late that Friday afternoon. She called to cancel her weekly Saturday night babysitting job with our family but her message was rather vague, so naturally I was curious about what was going on.

Later that evening I heard the news from someone else and was beside myself—sad, angry, upset, and extremely tearful. How could this be? Naomi was so young and beautiful. She had only recently returned from her trip to Germany and seemed perfectly fine and healthy. Why Naomi? It seemed terribly unfair.

Then Naomi visited me on Sunday—Mother's Day. It was a cloudy afternoon, and when I heard the knock I looked up to

Naomi's colored-pencil drawing of the woman and angel

see this beautiful, young angel with gorgeous long, blonde hair and lovely long, strong legs appear at my door. Immediately, I embraced Naomi, expressed my sorrow to her, and began to cry uncontrollably on her shoulder. With grace, strength, and tenderness, and without one tear, she consoled and comforted me. She assured me she would "beat" this thing and that everything would be all right. I felt like a child lost in the arms of a beautiful, motherlike angel. Who was the mother here? Was it not she who came to wish me a happy Mother's Day?

My experience as a herald of these ghastly tidings was miserable. To begin with, I was apprehensive about telling Kathleen of Naomi's cancer since she had difficulty enough coping with her own condition and was on prescription drugs. Living alone in an apartment in the public projects, she held a part-time job stuffing envelopes to supplement her Social Security disability payments. Mustering up my courage and with whatever tranquility I could find, I phoned her with the bad news. Kathleen, a longtime member of the Unity Church, immediately began calling everyone she knew to pray for her daughter.

It was no easier sharing the dreadful news with relatives and friends. Both Jean's parents and mine were stunned and asked what they could do to help. Many non family members who had developed relationships with Naomi were similarly affected. The members of the Bahá'í Faith community were shocked and began praying immediately. Knowing we needed all the prayers we could get, I welcomed them, as did Naomi. Although the bleak results of medical tests were telling us Naomi would soon die, this contact with people who loved her reinvigorated our belief in the human spirit, in miracles, and in turning impossible dreams into reality.

As word got around, our phone rang often, and it became a chore explaining our situation to all concerned. I took refuge whenever I could in my spiritual roots, beginning with the awakening I experienced when I was nineteen and a freshman in college at New Mexico University in Las Cruces, far from my home in Washington, DC. At that time I had fasted for a few days and, after browsing in the library and picking up a book of Hindu holy scripture called the *Bhagavad-Gita*, became enraptured reading it. I had been brought up without formal religious training, and now a whole new world of consciousness began to awaken within me. Shortly afterward, I was introduced to the Bahá'í Faith and felt the same strong pull of spirit. I became a Bahá'í that year and embarked on a lifelong spiritual journey. Bahá'ís believe the two main figures of the Bahá'í Faith, Bahá'u'lláh and the Báb, initiated a new dispensation for the present age. The Báb, the forerunner, announced a greater one to come and after only nine years of teaching, suffered martyrdom before a firing squad at the age of thirty-one. Soon afterward, Bahá'u'lláh, proclaimed Himself as the One foretold, fulfilling the short dispensation of the Báb. Feeling threatened by this new revelation, the Islamic leadership turned the government against Bahá'u'lláh and He was exiled. Held captive almost His entire life, He endured innumerable hardships while writing over 100 volumes of work. The religion He established spread throughout the world and is currently found in every nation. The overarching principles of the Bahá'í Faith are the oneness of God, the oneness of humankind, and the oneness of religion.

Now, every step of the way, my faith would be tested as Naomi turned to God for health and protection, and all of us who loved her clung to the hope that the merciful Lord would heal her. Our most immediate task was to decide how and where to begin treating Naomi's cancer. It was necessary to determine if we would pursue conventional chemotherapy or alternative treatments, perhaps even going to Mexico. My father's side of the family has several doctors, including his brother and two nephews who are orthopedic surgeons in Dallas, Texas. He immediately began gathering information from them, and by the time we returned to the cancer clinic we had been given the name of Dr. Werner Gerhardt, a well-known Dallas surgeon specializing in bone diseases. Advising us to pursue treatment wherever we chose, our attending physician reported that although scans showed there was no cancer in the brain, the biopsy was positive.

We decided on Dallas, where Dr. Gerhardt practiced and the hospital had a pediatric oncology floor, which our local hospital lacked. Subsequently, my cousin Ben convinced Dr. Gerhardt to squeeze us into his booked-up schedule.

Though I had never been one to cry much, I now cried frequently, both in private and on the phone. Falling on my knees alone in my studio one day, I begged the Lord not to take my daughter from this world so soon. Admitting that her death would bring many people together in a great outpouring of love, I pleaded to the Almighty for a different way to be given to unite people spiritually. During my prayer, I felt a spirit from a higher plane giving me courage and hope. Then realizing a terrible suffering was upon us that needed a remedy beyond our feeble powers, I asked the Almighty Lord's help. At that moment, I felt a spirit communicating to my higher consciousness that Naomi would feel pain but her life would not end. Relieved that she would continue to live, I arose from my knees fortified with faith to face the overwhelming struggle ahead.

For years I had felt the presence of angels that reside in God's other realms. When I was a twenty-two, during a summer break at the Maryland Institute, College of Art, in Baltimore, I moved to a small town in Maryland and rented a room in a YMCA. One evening while ending my prayers, I felt a change occur around me. I seemed to be wrapped in a hazy, otherworldly light, and suddenly the perfumed scent of a thousand roses filled my nostrils. Turning toward the one window in my little cubicle, I saw a shimmering light come down, pass through the wall, and then hover above me in the approximate shape of a person's aura. Immediately I knew I was in the presence of spirit and was frightened. The light shimmered in place, waiting for some acknowledgment, until with trepidation I said, "I am afraid. But come into me." Then it descended into my soul and for a few dazzling moments bestirred my whole being before vanishing. Powers exist beyond our mental abilities to understand, I thought. And so when my precious daughter came under attack, I began calling upon allies in the invisible realm, hoping for protection and assistance.

As we prepared for our trip to Dallas, I knew my life was forever changed. Not only was I intensively seeking spiritual assistance, but I was also beginning to feel what it is like to live with the presence of death. Worse, it stalked my daughter, who was more dear to me than anything. If I went dancing with Jean, worked in the garden, or simply rested in bed, its shadowy specter was there in the background, haunting my moments, pushing on my soul. Still, I clung to a belief that Naomi was protected by the mercy of God, who would deliver us from this darkness. A memory emerged of *Daniel in the Lions' Den*, a Rubens painting I had seen in art books as a child, depicting a supplicating Daniel, seated on a rock in a cave, surrounded by growling, ravenous lions. The painting made me realize that Naomi too was in an impossible predicament, but would be saved by God. I again thought of my dream years earlier of the shooting star and the warrior on horseback. I had always felt that because it was my dream, although the arrow hit the child, *it was my heart* and nobody else's. Now, gradually I realized the dream's foretelling of future events—of the pure spiritual strength directed into Naomi, perhaps because she was ready to receive this sacred gift.

Naomi, on the other hand, spent the days before our departure gathering strength for her battle, and already showing signs of a warrior. Despite the appalling strength of the enemy she was facing and the odds stacked up against her, she said, "One thing I need to do is to be happy and not let it get me down." Hearing these words reinforced my faith that she would be victorious in regaining her health.

DALLAS

*Dear God, I am scared, but I know that if I trust you
and spirit, everything will be okay.*

We decided I should go with Naomi to Dallas while Jean remained with Sarah in Santa Fe. On the day we left, Naomi walked with difficulty, and it hurt me to watch her limp painfully along at a slow pace to our gate at the Albuquerque airport.

Arriving in Dallas, we were met by my physician cousins, Ben and David Boone, whom I had not seen in almost forty years. Ben, the oldest, stood smiling in his blue jeans and black Harley Davidson T-shirt. He had a goatee, and his brown hair was tied back in a short ponytail. By his side stood David, forty-five, the same age as me. Trim, and showing signs of balding, he wore slacks and a pin-striped shirt. That night they took us with their girl-friends, out to dinner at a revolving restaurant on the top floor of a

Dallas skyscraper and afterward showed us around town. Although Naomi and I were stunned over our sudden predicament, and nervous about our fate, we relaxed when Ben and David began teasing each other. Laughter, as it turned out, was good medicine.

The next day, David took us to Dr. Gerhardt's office. After a brief wait, we were called into an examining room, where the doctor soon appeared, wearing a white physician coat with his name sewn over the breast pocket. Originally from Germany, he was middle-aged, of medium height with dark hair, and very bright. He had a thriving clinic and flew his own airplane. After x-raying Naomi and ordering a full array of diagnostic imaging exams, he advised us that the tumor had caused a fracture in her hip, which was in danger of breaking, so she needed to be on crutches. Looking concerned and not very hopeful, he added that perhaps after chemotherapy had shrunk the tumor, he could cut it away and then do reconstructive surgery.

When he left the examining room, I gazed with trepidation at the X ray on the light board, which clearly showed the monstrous aberration on Naomi's left side—evidence that crushed any faint hope I harbored that this was all a mistake. Soon a nurse came in and adjusted crutches to Naomi's height. Naomi held them awkwardly, as if unsure what to do with them, as I stood helplessly by, unable to extricate her from what was becoming a nightmarish existence. The medical establishment had given her only a 15 percent chance of surviving.

Subsequent exams further confirmed that a huge tumor weighing pounds had grown from her left hip into her abdomen area, pressing against the muscles and organs of her pelvis. Surgery was not an option because her hip could not be removed, and further, there were cancer nodules in twelve different places in her lungs. Fortunately, the bone scan revealed that the disease had not spread through her bones. Even though we were hoping the outcome of the exams would be more positive, Naomi confided that she had a foreboding prior to the scans that cancer was in her lungs.

When David met me outside the diagnostic imaging center

while Naomi was inside being examined, I hugged him and cried. It felt as though my world had darkened and the earth was but shifting sands. At a loss for words, he hugged me back, and although he could not take the pain away, I appreciated his being there for us.

Next, we went to the hospital's pediatric oncology offices to meet Dr. Andrew Breva, one of the two physicians who would oversee Naomi's chemotherapy. He tried to assure us, saying that there had been survivors among other patients who had been similarly afflicted. He also warned us of the side effects of the forthcoming chemotherapy, saying Naomi's hair would fall out, the linings of her digestive tract would be damaged, and she might become infertile. Furthermore, even if she went into remission, there was a 50 percent chance of relapse, in which case the cancer would be much harder to treat. Clearly, we were battling overwhelming odds. Naomi and I both cried, for we sensed the precipice we were on.

I flashed on a similar experience of helplessness I'd had when Naomi was seven years old. That summer, Jean, Naomi, Sarah, and I drove to Colorado to hike and camp in the mountains. While I hiked alongside Jean, with Sarah on my back, precocious Naomi clambered ahead of us up a rocky path for a view from atop a ledge. Watching her from below, I shouted at her to be careful and to not go any farther. But she continued to climb. Glancing up a few moments later, I watched in horror as she tumbled over rocks, fell through the air, hit a granite ledge, and then rolled to our feet with a broken arm. Now looking on in helpless terror, I again saw Naomi falling through the air, knowing that she would smash violently into hard rocks, the force of gravity and weight of her own body pulling her inexorably downward.

Dr. Breva gazed silently at us, having been through this situation before. Then he directed me to the business office to settle the first of what would quickly become a mountain of bills.

The next day, Naomi was admitted to the hospital and ushered to a room on the pediatric oncology floor, where we met Dr. Levi, the other physician in charge of pediatric oncology. A tall, slim man with black hair and a deep raspy voice that seemed to gurgle up out of his throat, he had a habit of gazing downward as he listened to people speak.

We were also introduced to the clinical nurse specialist in charge of meeting the needs of pediatric hematology/oncology patients and families. She gave us pamphlets to read, explaining more about procedures that would be undertaken during treatments. The treatment regimen for Naomi was called "very high-dose short-term chemotherapy for poor risk neuroectodermal tumors, including Ewing's sarcoma, in children and young adults." Naomi was considered at poor risk because of the large size of her tumor and the metastasis in her lungs.

Moreover, we learned from Dr. Breva that a tube called a central venous catheter would be surgically implanted in Naomi's chest, entering near her sternum, then snaking through a major artery leading to her heart. A port, which could be opened or closed, dangled at the end of the tube coming out of her chest, allowing blood to be drawn or drugs to be introduced into her bloodstream. Various potent drugs would enter her body this way—many with strange-sounding names such as Ifosfamide, Vincristine, Adriamycin, Doxorubicin, and Cyclophosphamide. Once in the bloodstream, the chemo drugs would either prevent the cancer cells from dividing or deprive them of a substance required to function, eventually destroying them. The drawback was that they affected not only cancer cells but also normal rapidly dividing cells, such as those in the gastrointestinal tract, bone marrow, and reproductive system. Because white and red blood cells would also be destroyed, Naomi's immune system would become compromised. As a result, I was required to sign letters of consent stating that I knew the danger of the treatments and that I agreed to them. Dr. Breva, understanding my anguish at the injury Naomi was facing, said, "These treatments are terrible, and a better course of action will someday be available, but unfortunately, this is all we know at the present time."

Later that morning Naomi was taken to the surgery unit to have the catheter placed in the artery leading to her heart. The surgeon, after introducing himself, immediately bonded with her as she bravely kept the conversation going until the preoperative medications made her groggy. While she was being wheeled to the operating room, the doctor looked warmly into my eyes and told me, "I'll take care of her. I have a son her age." After the operation, the port dangling at the end of the tube extruding a few inches from her chest remained a permanent fixture of her body until her treatments were over.

Chemotherapy was to begin at midnight. That afternoon, once Naomi had awakened from surgery, we began the wait for her treatment to begin. Large by hospital standards, her room had a filtered air system and an antechamber where visitors were expected to wash their hands before entering. In addition to the patient bed, there was a lounge chair that folded out into a makeshift guest bed. The view out the large bank of windows facing south was of the employee parking lot and a little grassy area along a parkway.

About 9:00 P.M., as Naomi lay down, I did also, still wearing my clothes. I felt anguish and apprehension as the minutes ticked by. While the light from the nurses' station filtered into the darkened room, and the ventilating system hummed, we talked a little, and then fell quiet. I felt deep sympathy for my precious daughter, and was baffled about why this suffering and hardship had befallen her. Moments later, Naomi asked if I would lie next to her, so I climbed into bed and held her in my arms, something I had not done since she was a baby. As I held her, I thought about what would happen to her reproductive system—how she probably would not be able to have children, even though she had said she always imagined herself as a grandmother. Now, as I lay next to my beloved daughter in her hospital bed, I opened my heavy heart to God, and said silently, *Because we love you, Lord, we accept whatever terrible circumstance we are in, and endure it for your sake, offering it back to you as a sacrifice.* Yet I could not help thinking that Naomi's suffering might be unnecessary since the awful treatments were merely a substitute for a cure. Surely a solution exists, I told myself, but where is it, especially now, when we need it? Then I felt a spirit descend and touch my soul with love and compassion, an otherworldly sympathy for our plight in the darkness of this world.

Naomi and I lay together for a long time, too uncomfortable to sleep yet not wanting to be apart. Then at midnight, a nurse entered the room, and after tenderly looking at us huddled together under a blanket, she put on rubber gloves and began fastening a bag of chemicals to the IV pole, saying gently, "Naomi, it's time to start." She then connected the line to Naomi's port, initiating the slow, steady drip of chemicals into her bloodstream. I moved back to the unfolded lounge chair, surprised by Naomi's composure at the start of this terrifying treatment. But although it was quiet and dark except for the light from the nurses' station, glancing frequently at Naomi trying to get comfortable, I could not fall asleep.

Chemotherapy treatments were given at very high doses four or five days at a time. Different combinations of chemicals were used on different days. As the medicines did their work, there was a steady drop in Naomi's red and white blood cell counts. The doctors waited while the counts dropped and then used stimulating factors called CSFs—hormonelike substances that regulate the production and function of blood cells—to promote the growth of infection-fighting white blood cells. When those cells had sufficiently increased after about two weeks, the chemo resumed. Following the treatments, Naomi would sometimes throw up and feel achy. Because her immune system was being severely compromised, it was necessary that she remain in her sterile room with constant monitoring. And because doctors feared contamination from bacterial mold, she could not touch or smell the flowers sent by well-wishers. Instead, she could only gaze at them through the window as they sat on the counter of the nurses' station.

The physicians had agreed on a radical program of high-dose chemo followed by radiation and a bone marrow transplant. The term "transplant" was confusing, since it meant that first, chemo was to be administered in such high doses that Naomi's bone marrow would be destroyed. The key to surviving this treatment was the timely reintroduction of small bits of living matter called stem cells, which would be harvested from her blood earlier and then frozen until the procedure began; this was the "transplant" part. These stem cells, after finding their way back into her bone marrow, would begin to reproduce blood cells again and multiply. Then hopefully, Naomi would recover with no remaining sign of cancer.

On the day of her stem cell harvest, a technician wheeled a big machine into the room, then unraveled clear tubing, inserting one end into Naomi's port and attaching the other to the machine. When the contraption started up and began spinning its drum, it made a groaning sound. Naomi reclined uncomfortably on her bed while a nurse and I stood next to her. When her port was opened up, a tiny bit of blood trickled out and then stopped. The nurse fiddled with the port, but the blood would not flow. Naomi, meanwhile, lay quietly on her side, speaking to her body in soothing tones, willing herself to relax until at last the blood flowed through the tube into the machine, where it was spun and then sent back into her heart. The moment I saw Naomi's blood surging through the clear tube, I felt faint and had to leave the room.

After Naomi's stem cell harvest, an excited Dr. Levi told us that the procedure had been extremely successful because about ten times the usual number of cells had been collected. I thought to myself that the vitamin B-12 injections she received in Santa Fe before coming to Dallas had surely helped. In the ten days between her diagnosis and our departure for Dallas, I had gone into deep meditation and found my intuition directing us to vitamin B. It occurred to me that vitamin B-17 would help, but I did not know of such a vitamin, so following further inspiration I came to vitamin B-12. Then intuition told me that large doses were needed—a shot a day for over two weeks. I resolved, despite my medical ignorance, to totally trust this vision. Eventually, despite my strange request and after considering her circumstances, a doctor gave her seven injections of vitamin B-12. Now, listening to Dr. Levi's report, I was almost certain the shots had helped boost Naomi's red blood cell activity and also helped sustain her through the very high doses of chemotherapy. With this, I began to trust in the visions that came during my meditations.

Fortunately, later lab results showed there was almost no chance of cancer in any of the harvested cells, which was important because they would be going back into Naomi. From now on, at selective times during her treatments, she would receive some of her stem cells back to assist in recovery. Previously, the doctors had only expected to gather enough to use for the bone marrow procedure at the end.

For a month, Naomi's hair remained intact and we thought perhaps she would keep her long, beautiful flaxen locks. But eventually her hair did begin to fall out, and right away she asked to have the hospital beautician cut it off. Minutes after he began working, she vomited, then apologized, but the stylist was understanding and commented, "My wife is getting chemo for her cancer now too!" Leaving about an inch and half of hair, he put the rest in a bag and handed it to Jean as a memento. But despite Naomi's touching attempts to care for her appearance, the hair that was left continued to fall out, covering her pillow each day until only a few wispy strands remained.

To encourage her healing, Naomi began a ritual of blessing each chemo treatment. Kissing her hand, she would pat the bag of medicine before allowing the nurse to let the dripping begin. She never explained her kiss, nor did anyone ask what it meant, but inwardly we all knew it was a sacred act and watched reverently while she sanctified the drugs and made them holy for her body.

Whether it was chemo, medicine for nausea, the antibiotic Bactrim, Mesna (a buffer to coat her bladder), or a solution to flush her out, it seemed Naomi was always tied to a pole holding bags that dripped fluids into her. Because buzzers sounded an alert whenever a bag emptied, sleep was impossible for more than few hours at a time.

Along with occasional visitors, mail arrived daily in bundles. Gary Myers, Naomi's high school art instructor, had bought postcards for his classes, and the students sent warm messages of love and support whether they knew her or not. Then Jean brought a package that made Naomi cry—a T-shirt signed by the entire track team, with messages of goodwill. Watching her break into tears as she held it up, I remembered how eagerly she had run with the team, how happy she had been when I picked her up after practice, how vigorously she had shouted encouraging words to her teammates during track meets. Now they were shouting encouragement to her, as if saying, "We are with you Naomi," "Keep going," "You are strong, and you will make it!"

Naomi was so moved by these messages of support that she wanted to respond personally to each one. I suggested a form letter. Instead, she was adamant about writing personally to everyone, despite the chemo sapping her energy. Holding to her word, each day she managed to sit up and handwrite notes until she had responded to everyone.

Everything I believed about health and well-being was turning on its axis. For instance, I had never put much stock in doctors, and now we were totally dependent on them. Until marrying Jean, whose father insisted on our family having insurance, I never had medical coverage, thinking instead my family would always be healthy, and that if any of us needed to go to a doctor, all the years of not requiring medical assistance and not paying premiums would offset any emergency expense. Now, with the treatments averaging over a thousand dollars a day, I was amazed our insurance company was paying such an astronomical amount. Our situation emphasized what little control people really have over their destiny. I desperately wanted to relieve the situation, yet the expenses made it apparent how little control I actually had.

In addition, I could not comprehend that Naomi's life might flicker and go out, but that possibility was constantly presenting itself. Now, at unexpected times, my hip hurt in the place where her tumor had grown. I figured these were sympathy pains letting me know I was closely bonded with her.

Faced with something like a broken bone, tonsillitis, or the flu, a confidence that healing will take place is comforting—we expect small mishaps to occur in life. Minor physical hardships are normal, and we are prepared to deal with them. But when calamity strikes, even people who plan for disasters can be destroyed by something as small as a germ. This is when we understand that the world is but shifting sand.

I thought of Jesus' words:

> Lay not up for yourselves treasures upon the earth, where moth and rust doth corrupt, and where thieves break through and steal:
> But lay up for yourselves treasures in heaven, where neither moth nor rust doth corrupt, and where thieves do not break through nor steal:
> For where your treasure is, there will your heart be also. [1]

I then reflected on Bahá'u'lláh's similar wisdom:

> Break not the bond that uniteth you with your Creator, and be not of those that have erred and strayed from His ways. Verily I say, the world is like the vapor in a desert, which the thirsty dreameth to be water and striveth after it with all his might, until when he cometh unto it, he findeth it to be mere illusion. [2]

I began to see that Naomi's journey was spiritual, the ultimate drama of the heart. She will need to find her strength, I told myself, and any weakness in her will be severely tested. Like a warrior on a battlefield facing overwhelming odds, she might doubt her powers to overcome, only to go deeper into her soul for courage, relying on God and every ounce of will to carry her onward.

From my new perspective, the fight itself appeared as gruesome and terrible as any that had been waged by grown men at war. The battle she was fighting was littered with the bodies of those who had tried for victory and failed. Disfigurement and death of human beings of all ages was everywhere—arms and legs, skin, feet, and organs were cut off and thrown away. In desperate efforts to thwart the enemy, vicious chemicals were used which hurt the friendly troops; anything to kill the ravenous foe and still survive. Doctors became veteran generals, standing behind the friendly forces and giving commands, but often shaking their heads at the enemy's tenacity. The groaning of the wounded was loud on all sides, as well as the wailing of families. Already I could see what a fighter Naomi was, and I had deep admiration for her valor and strength.

COURT OF THE GOOD KING
AND QUEEN

Fears are something we need to hold and face.
The more we push them away, the more
they hold on to us.

While Naomi was undergoing treatments in the hospital in Dallas, I stayed at my cousin David's home, a single-story house with a backyard swimming pool located in a quiet, upper-middle-class neighborhood ten minutes from the hospital. During the times when Naomi was in recovery between treatments, she and I both stayed there. Although he did serious work during the day as an orthopedic surgeon, at home David was lighthearted and fun loving, so we felt comfortable with him, his girlfriend Lori, and his two Irish setters, Amber and Maverick. We immediately established a good rapport, and soon it felt as if we had always been friends.

During treatments, despite being cheered by visiting family, Naomi was terribly uncomfortable. At times, because of mouth sores, nausea, and burned-up membrane linings, she could not eat. As a result, the doctors gave her nutritional support through her IV. Along with chemo, she was routinely given antibiotics, saline solutions, antinausea medicine, and blood transfusions to replenish her ravaged blood cells. Because her blood-clotting platelets were being destroyed, birth control pills were also necessary so that she would not get her period and bleed uncontrollably.

Nurses were ever present, performing a wide array of duties. Potent drugs were going into Naomi at very high levels, and she was constantly being flushed out with fluids intravenously, so someone frequently needed to help her get to the bathroom with her crutches and IV pole. At times, I could see her world shrinking drastically, until she was concentrating on just moving her hand to lift a cup of water, or on hearing a visitor speak to her. It seemed she was living only by tenaciously willing herself to stay alive.

I was shocked at the amount of chemical substance going into my daughter. My mother visited from California and likewise was awestruck by the treatment procedures, assuring me that it was "very high tech." Fortunately, Naomi was watched closely and surrounded by many loving people who gave her energy. The doctors visited every day on their rounds, offering encouragement, and nurses with a special affection that went beyond duty, brought gifts or tokens from their own homes, including favorite videos. One nurse who sometimes came in for a hug told Naomi that if the other patients had her attitude, they would be doing better. Another nurse occasionally brought her children to visit.

Despite her entire body aching inside and out, vomiting, hobbling on crutches with a tube going into her chest from an IV pole, and all her hair fallen out, Naomi hardly complained, nor was she despondent. She remained determined and ever hopeful.

After a couple of courses of chemotherapy, Dr. Levi palpitated Naomi's tumor area one morning and said that it seemed softer. She remarked that she could move her left leg more without pain—a positive sign. Likewise encouraging, the first tests to determine how Naomi was faring were excellent. The lesion in her hip was smaller, and the nodules in her lungs had been reduced in number from twelve to four. Naomi had met her first challenge successfully, and everyone was thrilled. After hearing the news, we left the pediatric oncology offices, and stepped into the elevator to go down to the lobby. As the door shut, and we were alone, Naomi broke out crying in relief. "I am crying because I am so happy!" she exclaimed.

During a break between treatments, her immune system was strong enough for a return to Santa Fe, where Naomi resumed classes at the end of the school year. Her teachers and friends were very glad to see her, although they had to adjust to how she had changed. Now the varsity letterwoman was bald and walked with crutches, carrying a backpack filled with schoolbooks across her shoulders. Also, she was fighting a terminal illness while simultaneously longing to be a normal teenager. So much had changed for her so rapidly that now a new self struggled to emerge. "Hardship is something that might make me stronger, and the best thing I can do for myself is *be* myself!" she wrote in her journal. "God is with me," she kept saying. "I just need to give it all to Him."

Back in Dallas, I was, as before, almost constantly at Naomi's side, leaving only in the evening to sleep at David's. We were in the fight together, and many times I was reminded that she was the better soldier. One day my moving around in her room became too much for her. "Dad! Quit pacing . . . please!" she barked out at me. I was embarrassed, because I hardly knew what my feet had been doing. I had been praying.

On a warm afternoon in June when Naomi's blood cell counts were high enough, we got permission to walk outside the hospital. As I pushed the IV pole, trying to keep the lines from getting tangled up, Naomi hobbled along on her crutches. Once outside, we sat on a bench under a spreading oak tree. The balmy air seemed almost harsh after the ventilated, temperature-controlled hospital environment. While we talked about the healing quest, she said, "Through all of this, I have prayed to God almost every day." Making an analogy to a fairytale, I replied that the cancer had made it seem as though an evil enemy had stolen her kingdom, exiling her and threatening her with a death sentence. Now she needed to find the kingdom of the good king and queen, who waited for her arrival to restore all she had lost to the evil one. Furthermore, the journey was arduous and fraught with danger at every turn. Sometimes dragons blocked her path, causing fear, or dark demons weakened her by piercing the armor of her spirit. She needed all her courage and strength to battle the formidable enemies attacking her unceasingly, and must always remember she fought for the good king and queen who would reward her. It was just a matter of time until Naomi, the brave knight, would make her way to their court, where they awaited her at the banquet table.

As we talked, a squirrel scurried up an oak tree, stopping every so often to listen and to nibble on the stems of green leaves, causing them to fall off and drift to our feet. Picking up several of the leaves, I saw they had little nodules attached to them, like tiny tumors. Then I realized that the squirrel was nibbling off only diseased leaves! I felt that we were in special company—the squirrel was acting for spirit, telling us that Naomi's disease was also being chewed away.

At this point, I was so certain of Naomi's healing, I suggested continuing her therapy close by, at the University of New Mexico Hospital, in Albuquerque, which had a Pediatric Oncology Department that was capable of continuing the treatments begun in Dallas—with the exception of her bone marrow transplant. But Naomi felt safer in Dallas, having bonded with the physicians and nurses there.

Despite my confidence, Naomi experienced heartbreaking moments of doubt about her survival. Once while we were out driving in Dallas, she confided that she was occasionally disturbed by the thought, "I am going to die!" repeating itself like a broken record in her mind. I was startled by her comment, but then, drawing upon my faith, I was able to reassure her that she would live and that doubts were normal.

At times in Santa Fe, our family was given books about cancer, including some about people who had experienced remissions and cures through nontraditional approaches. For example, a neighbor who had overcome breast cancer lent us a book that detailed case studies of individuals who had recovered from a wide variety of cancers after changing to a macrobiotic diet. Intuitively, I sensed that there was something to this, and I wanted Naomi to follow a macrobiotic regimen. One difficulty was in making a shift in our family's eating habits; another was that Naomi did not fully believe such a diet would cure her. But we did practically eliminate meat and processed foods, and cut down on dairy products. Convinced about the benefits of healthful elemental substances, I bought a wheatgrass juicer and began growing and juicing wheatgrass, but since it was not easy to ingest, sometimes it caused Naomi to be nauseous and even throw up. It is like chemo, I told her, but could make her stronger without harmful side effects. To my dismay, she was often exasperated at my "inspirations," but nonetheless said she appreciated my support.

Sometimes I could almost see two strong angels on either side of Naomi. But although I had absolute faith that she was being helped through prayer and the guardianship of a host of angels, I was continually frustrated by not knowing where to step next. The wounding from her treatments bothered me tremendously, especially since I was sure a better way existed. Certainly we could find it, and arrive at the court of the good king and queen. Naomi, by contrast, was a warrior in the heat of battle, fighting so hard that she was barely aware of her wounds.

SPIRIT OVER MATTER

Dear God, I want to tell you that I am thankful for my remarkable body. The joy in my soul has helped my body to know how strong it actually is.

Naomi's dreams during this time often reflected either her condition or her state of mind in some significant way. One dream was particularly noteworthy:

While at an outdoor market, she was drawn to a woman who had come with a special gift for her: a fruit with healing powers that she had selected from a plant nearby. The woman handed her the gift, but as Naomi held it, the fruit suddenly dropped to the ground. As it lay there, a crowd of people gathered about, clamoring for the healing fruit. Naomi then took another fruit from the plant but wondered if it had the same powers. Nevertheless, this one she put in her pocket.

In discussing this dream with Naomi, I felt a spirit guide had presented the gift. When I asked why she had not picked it up after it fell, she replied that she did not know, then pointed out that she had taken another and tucked it safely in her pocket.

Actively crusading for less harmful alternatives to the chemotherapy treatments and convinced she could be cured now by more natural means, I thought the dream was confirming the wisdom in this approach. After all, the benevolent woman had proffered a magic healing fruit . . . *but Naomi had dropped it!* Not wanting to challenge the tremendous effort she was making, or her successes, I kept my thought to myself. Yet her dream furthered my belief that an alternative existed, although admittedly I had no idea how to prove it.

Naomi finished her chemotherapy treatments toward the end of July and went for scans three weeks later. To everyone's great relief, the scans showed her lungs to be free of nodules and her hip lesion to be a shriveled-up mass. By all accounts, it looked like the enemy was being routed. The physicians proclaimed her response to treatment "excellent," and Dr. Levi concluded that with the bone marrow transplant, Naomi had an 80 percent chance of full recovery—a comment that, despite being positive, angered me because I believed it was just a matter of time until Naomi would recover totally.

I believed good results were to be expected for I refused to believe in statistics. "Naomi is not a statistic," I would tell anyone who would listen. "Spirit over matter," I would say, thinking, *If only everyone would believe this, the combined power of unanimous thinking would surely have tremendous effect.* But doubts persisted, based on statistical facts. For example, at one point Dr. Breva had said that Naomi would not be cured if a single cancer cell was left in her—meaning of course, that the cell would divide and multiply all over again. Yet I knew people with malignant tumors who had been cured without chemotherapy. Thus, I found myself thinking that having a few cancer cells was not bad, because a spiritually powerful person could help the body overcome them.

Once during a conference with Dr. Breva in the presence of my father, I said, "So what if you manage to kill all the cancer cells. There was a time when my daughter had no cancer cells and then got cancer!" Both of them looked at me incredulously, and my father asked, "So what is your point?" I could not really explain, except to say that the terrible beating Naomi was taking through chemotherapy could conceivably leave her in the place she was prior to getting cancer, only weaker. It seemed something more fundamental and spiritual had to occur.

At every turn, I seemed to encounter a variety of alternative therapies, each with its own adherents. I read a *New York Times* best-seller titled *Recalled by Life,* the story of prominent physician Dr. Anthony Sattilaro, who at the peak of his medical career experienced unbearable pain and found he was loaded with cancer that had begun in his testicles and spread to his ribs. He did not have long to live. After beginning traditional treatments and undergoing surgery, he found a macrobiotic community that believed he could heal himself and began helping him. Then, against his doctor's advice, he eventually abandoned invasive therapies to concentrate on his radical change in diet and lifestyle. Three years after his diagnosis, he celebrated his fiftieth birthday cancer free.

It was obvious that what worked—alternatively or conventionally—for one person did not necessarily work for another, which made sense from my perspective. A myriad factors existed, and even more that were unknown. I suspected that cancer was a result of physical imbalances and that somehow, just as sick animals in the wild know instinctively to eat the bark of a certain tree or nibble grass to get well, humans might lean heavily on the intelligence within each cell of their body to cure themselves. To bolster my beliefs, I sought guidance in the Bahá'í writings, where it says:

When highly skilled physicians shall fully examine this matter, thoroughly and perseveringly, it will be seen that the incursion of disease is due to a disturbance in the relative amounts of the body's component substances, and that treatment consisteth in adjusting

these relative amounts, and that this can be apprehended and made
possible by means of foods. It is certain that in this wonderful new
age the development of medical science will lead to the doctors heal-
ing their patients with foods. [1]

Certainly in cases of cancer, there *have* been many reports of remedy
through diet, I told myself. But medical science scoffs at such claims,
and in fact deaths continue, healthy diet or not.

My resistance to the doctors' recommendations for more chemical assaults increased as time went on. For all their efforts, I still
felt like Naomi was in Dr. Frankenstein's laboratory. I was tired,
even defensive, from the steady, monstrous barrage upon her body
which, although an attempt to save her life, was mutilating her.
Further, it seemed like a shot in the dark, because no one could say
these procedures were a foolproof cure.

When radiation followed by a bone marrow transplant was prescribed as the next step, I recoiled. I did not know how anxious
I had become. In my teen years, I had suffered similar anxiety
when in daydreams I saw myself trapped between two immense
steel walls that were slowly, inexorably, closing in upon me with no
escape. Moreover, my belief was that the cancer had been vaporized enough, and that the medical protocol being prescribed would
endanger Naomi's life. I believed she could strengthen and heal
without harsh treatments further jeopardizing her health.

At home, the anxiety I felt about the escalating therapy began
spilling over into our family life. Occasionally arguments would
erupt over Naomi's course of treatments and who should have
the final say about them. Since her lungs were now clear and her
hip lesion shrunken, my gut feeling was not to return to Dallas.
Thus far I had trusted my inner voice, risking looking like a
fool to believe angels were guiding my feelings. I shuddered at
the idea of destroying all her bone marrow, then trying to revive it,
and I knew that radiation would further damage her reproductive
organs and possibly lead to leukemia. My heart despaired at the
thought of watching rubber-gloved nurses dripping killing chemi-

cals into Naomi. If other people had survived cancer without toxic treatment, many examples of which appeared in the lay medical literature, I had faith that she would too.

But, I wondered, what if I am wrong? While we continued to believe that Naomi was protected and we could be guided by intuition and prayer to a safer outcome, other people had different beliefs about curing her and preferred to trust in science. Naomi said, "I need to be able to trust myself and feel that whatever my decision is, it is right." The conflict for me was stressful. I lost all interest in sex, dropped twenty pounds, and was not sleeping well, some nights not at all.

Naomi with two friends

Meanwhile, Naomi remained graceful, even buoyant, saying, "I don't want to be someone always feeling sorry for herself." And she didn't. She pursued her studies, made new friends, and assisted the coach at track meets. Her devotion to the team was apparent even though she could not run. But then, I knew she *was* running—in a race more difficult than around the grassy high school field—and so did many others. A lot of people had their eyes on her, silently cheering her on from the depths of their souls.

As for my own anguish, I drew consolation from Bahá'u'lláh Who, when speaking of redemptive suffering for the sake of God, had said:

> *Every vexation borne for love of Thee is a token of Thy mercy unto Thy creatures, and every ordeal suffered in Thy path is but a gift from Thee bestowed on Thy chosen ones.* [2]

Naomi kept so busy that she inspired people who were struggling with problems of their own. Every time misfortune knocked her down, she quickly got back up. In her journal she wrote: "I trust that God knows my love for life, and the happiness it gives me."

That summer during a break between treatments, Naomi went alone to Ocamora, a retreat center in a little village a few hours' drive from Santa Fe. I had encouraged her to take time to decide on her course of therapy and to do so through meditation and prayer, for she appeared to be swept along by violent currents and needing to catch her breath. Some of the people at Ocamora already knew her and were familiar with her situation. Embracing her into their nondenominational spiritual community, they formed a circle around her, and sent healing energy to her through thought. She prayed, meditated, and went on guided visualizations with a woman we had known for many years. Still using a crutch, Naomi also went on walks alone.

While she was gone, our family had little contact with her. I wrote a letter to the doctors in Dallas, outlining my belief that the cancer had been sufficiently vaporized and apparently was no longer visible in her lungs. Furthermore, the lesion in her hip appeared only to be a shriveled mass. Continuing harsh chemical treatments could drastically endanger her life; Naomi needed to strengthen and heal alternatively. Within days both Levi and Breva replied, emphatically stating their professional opinion that treatments must continue without delay.

To my chagrin, when Naomi returned from Ocamora, she said she had decided to continue the advised treatments. I was in turmoil about what might happen next and fiercely believed we could find a better way. Jean, however, supported Naomi in her decision, saying she strongly trusted that Naomi's belief in whatever treatment she received was paramount to its effectiveness.

My father, who had been phoning other physicians around the country, told me that the protocol used in Dallas was "cutting edge" treatment. I replied that the chemotherapy drugs were all carcinogens; Naomi's organs were being weakened, perhaps permanently; she had to be tested for heart damage; her hair had fallen out; she often needed blood transfusions in the hospital to stay alive; her reproductive system was demolished; and now the plan was to "up the ante" and give her radiation, which would effectively destroy her DNA and put her at risk for leukemia. Add to that the bone marrow transplant, which would essentially annihilate her bone marrow, and what would be left of her? This was cutting edge? I told my father that I would get second opinions and schedule more scans in Santa Fe. Surely, I thought, the scans will show her continuing to heal—proof that her body can mend itself now.

While I fought for solid ground, every step felt like the world was made of quicksand. Then I had a dream:

Late in the afternoon I drove into a mountain canyon that was very narrow and steep. For some reason my truck wheels were on the ground but the cab was up in the air, maybe fifty feet. I was sitting in the driver's seat looking at the stream flow down the canyon and under my truck. Suddenly I saw a young woman in a white cotton dress skipping from rock to rock along the mountain stream. She seemed happy and moved easily over the stones, passing underneath me and out of view. Then the perspective shifted, and I was at ground level again. When I looked downstream behind me, I saw Naomi curled up, lying still on her side in the middle of the icy cold stream, gurgling as if she were drowning. I ran to her and noticed she was barely conscious. Strangely, her eyes were distant and two little Pan-like horns were coming out of her head. I lifted her limp body and carried her home.

Waking up from this dream in the middle of the night, I was anguished. Was the future being revealed? The young woman had been skipping easily over the rocks along the stream and now she was immersed in the cold water, barely alive. I became increasingly concerned about the fate of my little wood sprite.

Naomi also had an important dream around this time:

As she stood by the front gate of a building, she saw guards dragging a man on his stomach through the courtyard. Feeling disturbed, she walked inside, only to be confronted by a man asking her to do something. When Naomi did not agree to do exactly what was asked, she was jabbed in the back by a sharp object and immediately went limp. The next thing she knew, she was wired throughout her body. The man who wired her had controls, and she was afraid of going to him because she felt she would be shot. Then she killed him, went to the control room, and had all the people who had been wired come with her to a place where there was a huge magnet. Then all the wires disappeared.

Hearing this dream, I thought, My God! She *has* been jabbed with a needle that made her numb. A wire *has* been implanted in her for others to control substances going into her body. She is afraid to say anything to them because she fears being shot down. And she longs to help everyone in her situation be free again. Perhaps the magnet was a Magnetic Resonating Image device—if this MRI showed her cancer was gone, all the wires would be taken out. But when I began to offer my interpretation, she quickly shut me off, reluctant to have me interpret her dream for her and equally unwilling to interpret it herself.

To get a second opinion about her future treatments, Naomi and I visited my middle-aged family physician, who practiced holistic medicine. After he briefly examined her, we all sat down to talk. The doctor listened while Naomi and I both spoke frankly about our perspectives on treatments. I expressed my hope to avoid more harsh chemicals, instead allowing Naomi to detoxify and carefully pursue alternative cures. Naomi, on the other hand, saying it was her decision, felt that she needed to continue with treatments advised by the Dallas doctors and to begin radiation. I wondered if Naomi, caught up in an intense battle and on the edge of death, was shell-shocked and unable to decide how to help herself. The doctor listened carefully, acknowledging our candor with each other and our close relationship, but he could not point us in any certain direction. To determine what had happened over the six weeks Naomi had not had treatment, I asked him to order scans for us at the local imaging center.

Comparing the new scans with the previous set, the radiologist reaffirmed that no cancer could be detected in Naomi's lungs and that the lesion on her hip was unchanged. Although somewhat discouraged that the hip lesion had not further diminished, I was relieved that at least it had not grown, since by its nature cancer spreads. Maybe it's dead, I thought. But all the radiologist could tell us was that it *appeared* to be dead, showing characteristics that experienced eyes hoped to see after such treatment. As much as I wanted to be certain that Naomi was out of danger, no one was prepared to tell us that.

Following the scans, Jean, Naomi, and I decided to meet with the chief physician of the pediatric oncology unit at the University of New Mexico Hospital in Albuquerque. He turned out to be a young, affable man, probably in his late thirties, with reddish hair. We had brought scans with us, from the earliest to the most recent, and the doctor put them on the light board so we could view them together. When he saw the original tumor, he exclaimed, "Wow, that is a whopper!" Looking at Jean and me, he stressed that the particular cancer afflicting Naomi was the "great white shark of childhood cancers," and needed to be attacked as aggressively as possible. When I suggested that less damaging therapies could result in a cure, he grew taut. Shaking his head, he emphatically endorsed proceeding with radiation. Looking at me, he said, "Another family had this conversation with me. They said they would go to India for an Ayurvedic cure for their child, and they promised to write me when he recovered. I never heard from them again!"

At that point, I realized it was useless for me to resist anymore, and accepted an appointment for us to see an Albuquerque radiologist. Then, as we were about to leave the pediatric floor, Naomi was invited to meet privately with another patient who also had Ewing's sarcoma. Danny was a thirteen-year-old boy who, like herself, was battling for his life.

A few days later, when we met with the radiologist, he told us cordially but firmly that Naomi had better get the prescribed treatment. Not long ago, he emphasized, no one in her situation survived. He explained that her reproductive system would be irreparably damaged, at least on the side that was being exposed to treatment, and possibly on the other side as well because of the scattering of rays. "It is either this or not do anything, in which case the cancer will kill her," he told us. Dismayed, because I felt alone in my faith that Naomi could now survive with natural remedies in lieu of radiation and chemicals, I signed the form stating that I understood the dangers inherent in the radiation, and consented to let it begin. Naomi would start treatments the following week.

During a visit with her mother for lunch at a restaurant, she connected deeply when Kathleen opened up her grieving heart to her and said, "You know, Naomi, I feel guilty about what you are going through; that I can't be with you!" Indeed, Kathleen had not been by her side during any of her treatments.

Naomi responded, however, with kindness and compassion, replying, "Mom, we're both adults. I love you and you love me. Love wins out in the end."

Resigned to follow the prescription of the medical establishment, I continued to have faith that Naomi would get to the court of the good king and queen, but felt she was taking a longer, more perilous path. Facing her difficult future with courage, Naomi wrote in her journal: "The only thing I ask of God at this point is reassurance."

NEW YORK

**You don't always have to search for happiness.
It is usually there.**

An uplifting interlude in this litany of painful events was a call from the Make-A-Wish Foundation informing us that Naomi had been selected as a "wish child" for New Mexico. This was a complete surprise to us, as we had no idea she was even known to that organization. Evidently her name had been submitted in Dallas by the pediatric oncology social worker, and upon reviewing her case the New Mexico chapter had decided to select Naomi as a gift child. Consequently, a wish granter from Albuquerque made arrangements to visit one evening and then appeared at our door with a magic wand and a bag of gifts for Naomi and Sarah. A tall, slender woman with long brunette hair, she was relaxed, and smiled as she introduced herself. Joining us in the living room, she sat beside Naomi on the couch. What an unusual experience this is, I thought, as our guest took gifts from a bag, handed them to Sarah and Naomi, and then waved her magic wand, saying, "Now, Naomi, think of anything you want—a trip, shopping spree, meeting someone special—and we will try to make your wish come true." Soon Naomi had come up with about twenty different possibilities, everything from a gazebo for our garden to an Alaskan cruise or a trip to the fashion district of New York City. She was told to think hard about her list in the next couple of weeks and choose what she most wanted. We were all excited, especially since the Make-A-Wish Foundation included the whole family in any travel plans. Thanking the volunteer, we promised that Naomi would call her soon. After she had left, it felt like somewhere in heaven angels were watching over us, and had sent one of their own to touch our lives with love.

Meanwhile, high school had begun, and Naomi was now a senior. We talked about whether she would wear a wig to cover her bald head, but her spirit was stronger than her vanity, and she was determined not to hide what she was going through. So she appeared on the sprawling campus bald but with a positive attitude. When I saw her scramble to get ready in the morning and then fly out the door to get to school on time, my heart leapt with admiration and pride. In so many ways she had become my teacher, not the least of which was how she strove to make the most of every minute given to her in life.

Soon the radiation treatments began in Albuquerque—about 55 miles away. Naomi's hip was to be radiated every weekday for six weeks and her lungs were to be treated for about three weeks. Fortunately, many neighbors and friends stepped forward to help with the driving, as well as my sister Laurel, who left her family in Alaska to be at her niece's side. The modern radiology center was in the midst of a mixed residential/business area. Entering the building on the first day, we went to the reception desk in the sunny waiting room, and from there we were ushered to a nurses' station. A young technician led us into the treatment room, which was windowless and empty except for a huge machine with its powerful lens focused on a steel table in the middle of the carpeted floor. Naomi was placed on the table in the barren room, with the mammoth machine over her. Lines were inked onto her stomach and then later, her back, marking places to be hit with the red light of laser beams projected from fixed stations in the room. During the course of her treatment the ink marks would stay as reference points, so that each time she visited, the laser beams could be lined up perfectly, and she would be in the exact position for the beam of radiation.

After Naomi was positioned on the table, the technician said, "Okay, Naomi, we are going to leave you in here alone now, but there is an intercom, so I will be talking with you and able to hear you also!" Leaving Naomi, the technician shut the door and we stood by the television monitor. Asking through the intercom if she was all right, and hearing her reply yes, the technician pushed a button and we heard a popping noise, made by the machine as it fired a current of painless radiation. Then Naomi was turned over and another dose was administered.

When we left the clinic that day, Naomi said, "To overcome my fear about radiation, I envisioned it as a stream of warm sunlight, sending healing rays into my body." After a later treatment she added, "Sometimes it is frightening. I ask God to help my body, because I know in the back of my mind that my body must be strong to deal with so much sunlight!" Again Naomi was sanctifying the deadly assault on her precious body—just as she did when she kissed her hand and patted the bags of chemo before it entered her bloodstream.

After a while, the ordeal of driving to Albuquerque, receiving radiation, and driving back to the house became routine. It was strange-Naomi leaving school early each day, driving home, and then making this two-and-a-half-hour round trip with a friend or family member for a procedure that took only a few seconds.

Bald and on her crutch, Naomi drew the attention of others and easily engaged in conversation with people; but when she went for treatment at the clinic, she liked to get it over with quickly and then leave. I noticed this about other cancer patients as well. It was as if they did not want to see the closeness of death mirrored back at them in the faces of others fighting for life.

One day while Naomi was being examined by the radiologist, he mentioned to us that another young patient's treatments were failing to stop his cancer. Naomi was deeply disturbed to learn that it was Danny, the boy she had met at the University of New Mexico Hospital. Climbing into the car for the drive home, she started to scream in rage. "I am really mad! I hate cancer! It's not fair!" I understood her outburst; she wanted Danny to be winning his battle as much as she wanted to win. I felt remorse for him and his family, but at the same time, relief that Naomi was recovering.

Later at home, Naomi wrote:

I am strong, and I think that being strong inside and out is important. Life is so beautiful I cherish it and want to be able to see every part of it. I know that I will because I am healing now.

Eventually we had to prod Naomi into resolving her plans for the Make-A-Wish Foundation gift. Seemingly ambivalent about accepting it, she asked, "Why me and not some other deserving child?" Despite her determination to live normally, she eventually gave in. Her eighteenth birthday—January 11, 1998—was just a few months away, after which she would exceed the age limit set by the organization. Because she had an avid interest in design and loved the excitement of big cities, she asked to visit the fashion district of New York and perhaps see some modeling shows. As it turned out, this was an unusual request that challenged the foundation's staff, since most kids wanted to go to Disneyland with their families. It was decided that we would take our New York trip at Thanksgiving, after radiation to the hip had been completed and before the lung treatments. We all looked forward to the excursion with great anticipation—not only as a way to lift Naomi's spirits but also as a means of maintaining family unity during these trying times.

At first, none of us realized what a fantastic adventure would unfold for us as a result of the Make-A-Wish Foundation gift. The local organization's staff scrambled to fulfill Naomi's wish, often working in tandem with the New York City chapter. Then as Thanksgiving drew near, we were astonished to learn of the lavish treatment in store for us. Besides being given spending money and reservations at the Grand Hyatt Hotel above Grand Central Station, we had appointments at two of the world's top design houses: Calvin Klein and Liz Claiborne. In addition, Naomi was asked to model one evening at a chic nightclub called the Fashion Café, owned by Naomi Campbell, Claudia Schiffer, and Elle MacPherson, three of the world's top models. Also, an evening on Broadway was arranged, with tickets to the wildly popular *Phantom of the Opera*. Our VIP status was further confirmed by tickets to the start of the annual Macy's Thanksgiving Day Parade.

After radiation treatments to her hip concluded, Naomi was given the okay to travel, and we embarked on our big trip. By now she had abandoned her crutch, searching the limits of her freedom. Because we were on an early flight to New York, it was arranged for us to stay in a Albuquerque hotel the night before our departure. We were happily surprised when, opening the door to our room, we found sparkling cider and treats, along with a colorful banner that read, "Have a great trip!"

Early the next morning our wish coordinator met us at the airport for a send-off. She gave each of the girls a camera, telling them that when we returned, she would develop the pictures and give them prints. Then she waved us off with tears in her eyes as we boarded our flight.

Jean, Naomi, and Sarah sat together, while I was a row behind them, next to a plump gentleman in his sixties with a thick European accent. He told me he was from Poland and had come to the United States after World War II. He had married, raised his family, and was now comfortably retired. Pulling up his shirtsleeve, he showed me a tattoo on his arm that was just numbers. I had seen this kind of tattoo before, and knew it was from a Nazi concentration camp. We then spoke about the Holocaust and his survival in the death camp. I glanced in front of me at Naomi, with her hat covering her bald head, and whispered to him that my daughter was trying to survive her own holocaust. Surprisingly, he said, "Yes, I saw that right away." Immediately I knew that this man, having lived through the "valley of the shadow of death," would never forget the terror, and I could barely fathom Naomi's innocence as she played cards and laughed with her sister in the seat ahead of me.

When we arrived in New York, a limousine driver holding a sign that read "Boone" awaited us at the baggage claim area. Retrieving our luggage, he loaded it into the car and drove us across town to the Grand Hyatt. It was thrilling finding ourselves suddenly in mid-Manhattan, among the skyscrapers and glittering streets.

The following day, a Make-A-Wish staffer met us at the hotel and took us by taxi to the Calvin Klein design house. There we were cordially greeted by a young woman who spent all day escorting us through the entire eight-floor operation. Simple formality was evident everywhere, with walls white, furniture black, and all company employees dressed in black. We met the heads of various departments, including advertising, design, and fashion, and each showed us their current project. The head of the Advertising Department joined us at lunch for a private, catered meal, then at the end of the day, a limo took us to the flagship store on Madison Avenue, where Naomi modeled some very expensive clothing, including an elegant evening gown. After the saleswoman blithely adjusted the front to cover the port dangling from her chest, Naomi stepped forward smiling and awkward, balancing on three-inch high heels to everyone's admiring gaze. Then before leaving, we were showered with gifts, which the staff promised would arrive at our home shortly after our return.

Another Make-A-Wish Foundation volunteer met us that night at the hotel and escorted us to the Fashion Café, where we would have dinner and Naomi would make her debut as a fashion model. A tall, svelte, black model who oversaw operations took Naomi aside as if they had been friends for years. Downstairs in the dressing room, she taught her how to saunter onto the runway, stride along to the end, twirl, look at the crowd, and then walk back. After they practiced together, the model, ignoring the port and Naomi's very short, half-inch-long hair, put makeup on Naomi. The rest of us, meanwhile, sat upstairs in the crowded, noisy café, waiting for the show to begin and eating appetizers at our table next to the runway, amidst large posters of models and blaring pop music.

At last the show began, and to the sound of booming, rhythmic music, several slim young women appeared, modeling fashions under the colored lights above the runway. We sat on the edges of our seats anticipating Naomi's appearance. After the third model had stepped down off the runway, the special guest model of the evening was introduced: "Naomi Boone, courtesy of the Make-A-Wish foundation, all the way from Santa Fe, New Mexico!" Striding to the end of the runway, Naomi hesitated, smiled out into the crowd, then turned and sauntered back while people applauded. A handsome, young, energetic employee grinned and then shouted, "Yeah, Naomi!" Wearing the newest fashions, she looked modern, even avant garde, with her boyishly short hair. Carefully stepping down off the runway, conscious of her weak left leg, she then disappeared to change into her next outfit as the other women came back out in their new attire. Naomi fit right in with the models, walking the runway five times in various outfits to cheers and applause. At the conclusion, Sarah was called over and asked if she would like to walk the runway. Sarah, eleven years old and wearing a faux-leopard skin dress she had put on that evening, immediately said "yes." Without a hint of trepidation, she too walked the runway down and back. Returning to our table, she sat down, eyes sparkling with excitement. Moments later, Naomi joined us for dinner—happy, and yet relieved that her modeling was over.

Naomi modeling at the Fashion Café, New York City

The next day, Sarah, Naomi, and I visited the Liz Claiborne design headquarters at Fifth Avenue and Broadway while Jean rested. I was continually amazed that Naomi, despite being in the battle of her life, was always the first one out the door to an activity and the last one to want to leave. Whereas the Calvin Klein design house had been stark, simple, and elegant, Liz Claiborne was more homespun and casual. As soon as we were greeted, we enjoyed a catered breakfast with a group of staff members and design professionals.

An assistant to the CEO escorted us through the organization from top to bottom. The designers told us how they brainstormed together to arrive at new fashions. Top fashion designer Dana Buchanan gave Naomi a signed original drawing. We were also taken to the showroom, where department store buyers came to see the newest line of clothing and housewares before placing orders. Eventually, we arrived at the office of the tall, amiable CEO, who received us graciously and invited Naomi to sit beside him at his big executive desk while I took pictures.

Our biggest surprise came when we were told that Naomi's name would appear throughout the evening on the huge electronic Liz Claiborne billboard at Times Square. We were invited to return the following day to view the Macy's Thanksgiving Day Parade from the catered comfort of the chief executive's office.

We had dinner that evening with our volunteer and her fiancé at an Italian restaurant. Leaving our hosts, we later walked to Times Square where, amidst crowds and glitter, we saw the huge Liz Claiborne billboard scrolling, "Welcome to New York, Naomi Boone!" then "Welcome Boone family—Steven, Jean, Sarah, and Naomi," and finally "Happy Thanksgiving." We lingered, then continued on to the Majestic Theater on West Forty-fourth Street, where we had tickets to the popular, long-running *Phantom of the Opera*. As we stood in line waiting to be admitted, we heard various languages spoken among people from all over the world. Once inside, Naomi was dismayed at having to climb so many stairs to our upper balcony seats with her gimpy leg, but she succeeded. Then as the lights went out and the music started, we were entranced in the magical realm of theater, reveling in the luscious drama of a spectacular production.

The next day we returned to the Liz Claiborne building to watch the Macy's Thanksgiving Day Parade. Security people checked our names off the guest list, and we went up to the eighth-floor office, where a small group of people had gathered. From there we watched as the parade passed below us, with crowds lining the streets for as far as we could see. Naomi and Sarah took pictures of the floats, marching bands, and huge cartoon balloons. The day was particularly windy, and we watched aghast as the Pink Panther balloon caught a breeze at an intersection, then dragged the handlers along before hitting a light post, which ripped a hole in its side. As the gigantic balloon began wildly deflating, several men quickly stabbed more holes in it to avoid losing control of its flight. After the parade, we returned to the hotel, clinging to one another as we passed through the throngs of pedestrians.

We had a sumptuous Thanksgiving dinner with our volunteer and her fiancé at the restaurant in the Grand Hyatt Hotel. Beforehand, she spent a few moments speaking with the manager, then came back to our table and announced we were being treated to dinner.

Friday we took the subway uptown to the Metropolitan Museum of Art, and later strolled around the zoo in Central Park, stopping to watch the seals do tricks as the zookeepers threw them fish. That evening we went to an upscale restaurant called Sign of the Dove. When we were escorted to our table, we were delighted to find waiting for us a dozen long-stemmed pink roses. Taking our seats among the well-heeled clientele, we eased into the cozy and romantic setting. Gazing at my lovely daughters and beautiful wife, aglow in the soft candlelight, I felt grateful for the kindness of strangers who had showered us with loving care and had afforded us shelter from the storm raging in our lives.

Saturday we met with my family members at the hotel. My brother Jed, his wife Diana, and their three-year-old son Kirby drove in from the suburbs, and my brother Wade arrived by train from Washington, DC. We rejoiced to see one another, especially since the girls had never met their nephew Kirby. Together, we all went to the Soho district to browse the art galleries, have lunch, and enjoy our long overdue visit.

The next morning our limousine driver took us back to the airport for our return to New Mexico. On the way, it was Naomi who commented, "After the difficulties we have been experiencing, it was great to just have fun and be treated like celebrities."

Soon after arriving home, Naomi wrote a particularly poignant note about her life: "I have gotten to the point where, for at least five minutes a day, I am filled with a wonderful sense of happiness. It is an indescribable sense of utmost freedom and joy. When I am in touch with it, I just think, 'Oh God, thank you for this beautiful body and life.' I have learned how to use 'thank you' throughout everything."

DANIEL IN THE LIONS' DEN

Do not be fearful—
sing, for fear only increases illness.
Be joyful! Laugh! Be joyful! When you feel fear, let it
come and go, then remember the joy!

At the beginning of December 1997, Naomi began radiation treatments to her lungs. She also started reading a book about listening to what our bodies tell us through dreams and physical manifestations. One night she asked her body to speak to her, and the next day she fell ill. Remarkably, from the beginning of her treatments, Naomi had never been sick except for some immediate harsh reactions to chemotherapy and radiation; now she came down with bronchitis. As a result, radiation in Albuquerque was delayed by a week. The radiologist was concerned and hoped we would keep to our schedule in order to get the benefit, and not just the side effects of the procedures. Meanwhile, I was continually frustrated about these treatments that were so hard on Naomi, wishing she could get well without them.

When Naomi was recovered enough to travel to Albuquerque again, she resumed her treatments until they were finished. A physical exam and blood test subsequently showed her to be fine except for a slightly suppressed immune system. The doctors in Dallas ordered new scans, and now feeling considerably more hopeful, we went to the Diagnostic Imaging Center in Santa Fe.

Two days later, as I was driving home late in the afternoon, Jean and the girls appeared along the curving road from the opposite direction. We stopped our cars side by side, and I could see something was wrong, because Sarah was crying and Naomi would not look at me. Jean and I both rolled down our windows, and when I asked what was wrong, she said, "The doctors reported that cancer has reappeared in Naomi's lungs." Speechless, we sat in silence a moment, then saying good-bye, they drove off. Dumbfounded, I experienced the same feeling of disbelief as when we first learned of the cancer—that it must be a dream. I could not comprehend this sudden turn of events.

While continuing down the road, I pondered our fate, for I had become accustomed to victories, having had no bad news since Naomi's original diagnosis. It felt like the solid ground of faith beneath me had opened, and trembling at the edge of a deep, dark fissure, I knew death had arrived. What had I been believing in? Had I been a fool, like a dowser walking slowly with his divining rod over parched land, praying for signs of water, attentive with every nerve until a tug filled him with jubilation and he announced with confidence, "We can dig here—there is water," only to find after much effort that nothing existed? What if I had been feeling merely my own longing? Or *was* there water and we had not dug deep enough? Arriving home, I walked the fields around our house and talked to God, saying, "Lord, I need to be able to trust my inner senses once again. I've lived by my intuition and faith. I need to believe my intuition!"

That evening we were all in shock. Naomi cried, curled up motionless on her bed in her dark room. I knew she was struggling to find the strength that she depended on and now needed more than ever. Simultaneously, I was gripped with helplessness and despair, wondering if all our efforts had been for naught and Naomi's determination futile. I cried inside, "Lord, where are you? Where is your shielding mercy? Where is your healing might? Why are you letting this happen to Naomi—especially since we have faith and confidence in you?" When dinner was ready, Naomi came to the table looking terribly sad, but I could see she had already found strength within herself and was gearing up for further struggle.

A letter from the radiologist arrived the following day. It stated that there were two nodules in the lungs, where before none had been visible, and that the hip appeared unchanged. A few days later, Jean spoke on the phone with Dr. Breva, who declared it was "regrettable" that treatments had been delayed while we were pursuing second opinions. Naomi, aware of this comment, said, "Dad, maybe we should not have waited to begin radiation." I felt bad and then reminded her that radiation had not helped Danny, the boy she met in Albuquerque at the cancer clinic. Who could say for sure what had happened? All we knew was that her lungs had been clear in the previous two scans and now the cancer was returning. It felt like we had tasted freedom, only to be hurled back into a miserable prison. Oppression like a plague was upon us. Now I knew the pain of existence as never before, and it caused my heart to flow with compassion for every being unfairly treated by the chances of life. Searching for words to bolster Naomi's spirit, I told her, "We are not beaten."

Naomi was scheduled to return to Dallas for more chemotherapy in January, followed by a possible bone marrow transplant. In the intervening weeks I had another portentous dream:

Two surgeons were leaning over a patient, performing an operation. They extracted some of the patient's cancerous tissue, mixed it with a protein, and then put it back into him to effect a cure.

I woke up excited about my discovery yet dismayed that I had no way to learn more about such a procedure. Perhaps it is performed somewhere in Asia, or belongs to the future, I reasoned, finally resigning myself to the fact that this information could not possibly apply to our present circumstances.

At times Naomi felt as if hope were slipping away, and that death was imminent. She wrote, "The future does not seem to be there." Nonetheless, she used her great strength to forge onward. Keeping positive, she finished the first semester of her senior year with good grades.

The holidays arrived, and Jean's entire family joined us in Santa Fe, enhancing our feeling of unity and support. Jean's brother Tom and his wife Barbara had brought their young children, Annie and Ben, who were slightly frightened because they had been told that Naomi might die due to her illness. It was scary for them to think that their steady and trusted playmate, whom they loved and adored, and who was so young and beautiful, could soon die. But shortly after their arrival, the young children no longer looked at Naomi with big wondering eyes, and instead enjoyed their nearness and pleasure at being together again.

Santa Fe is one of the most enchanting places in the world to enjoy Christmas, and we looked forward to the uplifting festivities. On Christmas Eve, all along the snow-covered streets in the old eastside art district, people set out thousands of farolitos— little paper bags filled partially with sand to hold a lit candle. Casting warm, flickering light along sidewalks and curbs, they dazzle the eye and warm the heart. Beginning at dark, streets are closed to traffic, and throngs of revelers stroll, stopping to sing carols by bonfires ablaze in driveways or side streets. The experience was breathtaking, as we all walked the streets together singing.

At the beginning of January, Naomi and I returned to Dallas, where David once again invited me to live at his house while Naomi went back to the hospital. Soon the rounds of chemo began again— this time with Cyclophosphamide and Topotecan. Trying to be encouraging, Dr. Levi told us about a young man whose cancer had come back after initial treatments but then had "melted away" in response to these drugs.

During the days, Naomi read, answered letters and E-mail, and sent instant messages to friends via the Internet, especially her buddy from Waldorf school days, Alexis Diaz—a constant companion throughout the ordeal. Simultaneously she grappled with the changes rapidly occurring in her body. One day while she was an outpatient and staying at David's, she began sobbing, tired of fighting for her life and afraid of her body's deterioration. Not only did her back, lungs, and head hurt, but also she had been coughing up blood and her hair was falling out for the second time. In tears, she grabbed crayons and paper and drew angry pictures. I also was anguished, feeling despair at my overwhelming powerlessness. Remembering the image of *Daniel in the Lions' Den*, I knew that all we could do was hang on and trust.

The next day, Naomi and I went to a barbershop to have our heads shaved. Naomi told the barber her hair was going to fall out anyway because she had cancer and was getting chemotherapy. I could see he was moved as he set his clippers to the lowest setting and began shaving. For years people had remarked how alike we looked, and now, after our haircuts, we looked almost identical. I felt solidarity with her, but sadly I realized that I had a choice about the matter and Naomi did not.

When Naomi's blood counts were high enough, we would often do something fun, like go to dinner and a movie, or watch TV and eat popcorn with David and his girlfriend, Lori. David's joviality provided a refreshing counterpoint to our tensions and anxiety. Yet despite such pleasurable interludes, the battle was ever present.

One day, as I was driving to a video store with Naomi, she suddenly dropped the morning newspaper on her lap and began to cry. Startled, I pulled over to the curb and asked what the matter was. A minute or two passed before she could answer. "On the sports page there are high school track and field pictures with stories." Knowing she longed to run again and struggling with my own tears, I told her to think of herself as someone who had been given a greater challenge in life than running track, which after all was only child's play compared with the race she was in. Then I reminded her of how proud I was of her, and that I shared her anguish. I hoped my consolation was helpful.

I again read the *Bhagavad-Gita*—the Hindu epic of the mortal Arjuna's crisis of faith on the battlefield, and Lord Krishna's divine insight into the value and purpose of struggle—and gathered courage from its wisdom, which seemed to address our own challenges in verses such as the following:

> *Feelings of heat and cold, pleasure and pain, are caused by the contact of the senses with their objects. They come and go, never lasting long. You must accept them.*
>
> *A serene spirit accepts pleasure and pain with an even mind, and is unmoved by either. He alone is worthy of immortality.[1]*

Reflecting one day on the importance of a serene spirit, I was reminded of a "gift" dream that came to me eleven years earlier:

> *A man had been castaway at sea in the darkness of night, and I sensed that a girl also was lost but I could not see her. The man was calm and knew he would die. A shark was nearby and the man spoke to it, saying, "Come, I am here. You may have me." The shark moved closer amidst the rolling waves, its great black fin protruding above the water. "But I am moving slowly; something might happen to you first," was its reply. Then the fin came dangerously close to the man as he bobbed helplessly in the waves.*
>
> *At that moment, I hoped the slaughter would finish quickly and not leave the prey alive, to be eaten piece by piece. Then suddenly, the huge beast rolled on its side, baring its frightening row of jagged teeth, and I knew the victim would be cut in half rapidly.*
>
> *Soon, people were gathering on the shore to make offerings on behalf of their friend who had died at sea. A house on the beach had*

a room where each person placed sacred objects on a shelf. A cord was then wound around each object, connecting it to the others, and all the people sang songs and spoke in honor of the deceased.

Later, one gentleman took me aside to explain that he had known the departed. He said that the man had listened intently for a long time to learn the "code of the sea" and had finally been transformed—forever to stay in the realm of knowledge.

It seemed Naomi and I were in the dark matrix of creation, being tossed about in deep, dangerous waters while facing an uncertain future with the great shark of death nearby. But a code existed that could transform our terror into calm, our anxiety into peace, and our fear into certitude. This was our quest—to learn the code.

JUST LET GO

*I was thinking of death today. I was thinking it is
not death I fear, but rather losing life and people.*

In the course of the recovery period from chemo, we returned to
Santa Fe, where Naomi resumed high school. The yearbook was
being organized, and like some of the other seniors, she and a
friend pooled their money to buy a full-page spread for themselves
in the back. When the photographer began taking pictures of the
students, Naomi, entirely bald, posed uncomfortably but bravely,
wearing neither a hat nor a wig.

Soon afterward, she had a revealing dream that would help her
to learn the code:

> *She was in a spaceship with two other people. They were trav-
> eling through space, and something happened that required her to
> open the door. When she did, there was a strange animal floating*

outside the spaceship. She tried to pull it in, but it drifted away. Then a horse with fingers flew by, and she grabbed one of them. As she held on to it with all her might, the horse said, "Don't be silly, just let me go!" Then she realized she needed more oxygen, and someone pulled her back into the spaceship.

The message of the horse, that everything was all right and she could "just let go," would assist her in the days ahead.

On January 11, Naomi's eighteenth birthday, Jean organized a surprise party for her at the home of Barbara Miller, Naomi's former Waldorf school teacher. To keep her suspicions at bay, our family pretended to be going to dinner at Barbara's house. When we arrived, the house was dark, and I acted as if perhaps Barbara and her husband Preston had not remembered we were coming. Then Barbara answered our knock, letting us inside, whereupon the lights went on and a cheer went up for Naomi. Among the well-wishers were many fellow students, friends, neighbors, and teachers. At first Naomi seemed stunned to be the center of so much affectionate attention, but then she smiled and looked around at all the familiar faces, acknowledging each person who had come to celebrate. When her cake was presented to her, she made a wish, took a deep breath, and blew out all eighteen candles. Later, after the crowd had thinned, she sat with her teenage friends, reminiscing about their old school days. Watching them laugh and talk excitedly among themselves, I felt a bittersweetness, aware that each of these young women on the verge of adulthood faced promising futures except Naomi, whose days ahead were far from certain.

In February we returned to Dallas, where scans revealed that there had been a 40 percent reduction in the visible cancer in Naomi's lungs. The doctors, encouraged that the cancer was still responsive to chemotherapy, scheduled a bone marrow transplant immediately. This was the procedure I dreaded the most. Naomi would need many transfusions, and we would wait anxiously to see if her stem cells that had been harvested and frozen a year earlier would revive her bone marrow once it was destroyed.

As soon as Naomi was settled in her room, the chemo treatments began anew, this time with high doses of Melphalan, VP-16, and Carboplatin. The bags were brought in by a nurse wearing rubber gloves and a mask, and were hung on the IV pole. As usual, Naomi blessed and kissed them before the contents began dripping into her.

Distressingly, each day I could see her getting a little weaker and struggling more. While her cell counts were still high enough to prevent compromising her immune system, she was able to walk the halls of the isolated transplant floor for short periods. On one such walk she met Jason, a tall, stout teenager her age who had leukemia. He also was a bone marrow transplant patient, but because his blood was affected, he could not be given his own stem cells, so instead, his younger sister with the same blood type had become his donor. Later, while I was eating dinner under the fluorescent lights of the family waiting room, a middle-aged woman with bleached blonde hair came in with her tray, and barely glancing at me, sat down. I could tell she was shielding herself, being strong on the outside while inside she was vulnerable and in pain like me. After a few moments I learned that she was Jason's mom, and had met Naomi. Talking while we ate, she said, "Jason had Hodgkin's disease when he was twelve, and was treated with chemo and radiation. Recently, he complained of constantly feeling tired at his hospital job, and a nurse urged him to get a blood test and a checkup. The results showed he had leukemia."

"Maybe from the radiation," I said.

"Yes, but he had a lot of cancer at the time. What else could we do?"

"Naomi has had quite a bit of radiation, too," I replied, commiserating with her.

Then she said the doctors had given Jason only a 50 percent chance of survival. I replied, "The doctors told us Naomi's chances were less than 50 percent." Taking a bite of food, I reminded myself that regardless of percentages, I had faith that she would live.

I mentioned to Jason's mother how strong prayer could be, thinking of all the people who regularly prayed for Naomi. She replied, "Yes, our entire church is praying for Jason." We both agreed to pray for each other's youngster.

After meeting in the hallway, Naomi and Jason began corresponding by E-mail from their rooms. One afternoon Jason shared his feelings about his present situation, his college plans, life in Dallas, and hopes for recovery. He wrote the following:

> *I'm gonna try to start classes in the fall if I feel well enough. I'm studying computer systems technology. (That's my major.) I wanna get a job in the computer industry. And nothing is gonna hold me down! Especially this little disease I have. As far as my job goes, I work in the Radiology Department. I am a radiology assistant, and I do things like develop X rays, go get people from their hospital rooms with a wheelchair, and bring them down to get a CAT scan or X ray or whatever. It was weird because one day I was taking people who were sick to get X rays, and the next day I found out I was sick. Ironic, huh?*
>
> *It's been three weeks and four days since I've felt a cool breeze of fresh air against my face. I wish you good luck, and I hope your "little stem cells" start growing!*

In this stage of Naomi's treatment, the stakes had risen considerably, and a sense of anxiousness had set in. The procedure had to work since there would be nothing else to follow it. As Dr. Breva promised her, "No more chemo. This is the last time."

As the days passed, Naomi became increasingly ill and weak. She focused intensely on maintaining a semblance of balance, concentrating on each little task. At first, visitors could go in and out of her room freely; but as her immune system rapidly weakened, strict limitations were imposed to protect her. Only two people at a time were allowed in the room, and both had to wear masks.

Almost continuously nauseous, Naomi ate only by sheer determination. Eventually, just the sight of food made her nauseated. And because everything hurt, she had to be given pain medication along with the antibiotics, antinausea drugs, saline flushes, and intravenous nutritional supplementation. The whites of her eyes became bloodshot, and her stools were bloody. She was being blasted.

To show family support, my brothers visited—first Wade from Washington, DC, who helped Naomi fill out a application to the Rhode Island School of Design (RISD), then Brent from Santa Barbara, California, who did crossword puzzles with her. She also began working on drawings to accompany her college application form. She had had her heart set on attending RISD ever since her visit there in the summer of her freshman year. At this critical juncture, I encouraged her not to attempt the difficult application, explaining that it could wait, but she was determined to pursue her dreams. Her talents were as strong as ever while her body was reeling. Naomi had loved making fine line drawings, often of invented faces, and her hand was steady and confident. Now I worried, for she was losing strength and the simplest tasks were becoming monumental.

Then one morning when Naomi sneezed, her nose began bleeding profusely. Tilting her head back, she choked on the blood going into her throat. Her platelet levels were so low that her blood could not clot. The bleeding persisted, and an ear, nose, and throat doctor was summoned. He placed swabs with artery-shrinking medication in her nostrils until the bleeding was finally checked. This helped for a while, but it was very uncomfortable, and when the swabs were taken out, the bleeding resumed. This frightening situation went on for three days until finally, after several platelet transfusions, the bleeding stopped.

When Naomi's cell counts showed that her bone marrow had been destroyed from four days and nights of continuous chemotherapy and was no longer effectively producing red or white blood cells, her thawed stem cells were given back to her. Jean and Sarah had come to be with us and helped Naomi make a poster, which they hung on the wall; it said, "Welcome Back, Baby Stem Cells!" Naomi blessed the cells that had been removed from her body months earlier and gave them pep talks, cheering them on to find their way back into her lifeless bone marrow and begin regenerating. She also wrote them a touching healing note: "May your journey through my body prove to give me strength and the essentials for total health! I see you attaching yourselves to my bones and growing up to be mature and hardworking cells. I love you guys!" Then she wrote, "Thank you, God, for the opportunity I have been given. Thank you for the chemo that is now in charge of releasing any last cancer cells that don't need to come back to this body again. Thank you for my healthy baby stem cells! My body is ready to nourish them."

After the transfusions, we waited anxiously for days and at last celebrated that there was a perceptible shift upward in her counts. Naomi said, "My focus now is to be rid of the cancer—release it into space, never to come back again." Movingly she wrote, "I want to show God that I have learned much and feel as though I deserve miles of life to unfold for me. I love this life, and I want to be here for as long as God allows. I trust that God knows my love for life and the happiness it gives me."

In almost record time, her counts climbed high enough for her to leave the hospital and return to David's house. There she continued with injections to stimulate her bone marrow's production of blood cells and took the antibiotic Bactrim to prevent infection. David made us feel at home. It helped that he was a doctor, and as always, his jovial nature was good medicine.

For weeks Naomi reeled from the chemo. Three or four times a day she vomited violently, so we kept a bucket and towel handy for the unexpected attacks. As usual, she tried to focus on life outside herself and to not dwell on her problems. She forced herself to eat and keep a positive outlook, using every skill she knew to persuade her body to recover. During the days, we worked on art together—I painted, while she produced more drawings for

Naomi's pencil drawing of an imaginary place

her application to college. RISD required three 16 by 20 inch pencil drawings: a bicycle or any part of it, an interior, and a subject of the applicant's own choosing. For the subject of her own choosing, Naomi made an exquisitely detailed drawing of a path leading into a leafy forest. Along either side stood columns supporting basins that overflowed with flowers. Marking the spot where the path split in two was a sign pointing in each direction. The scene was serene, astonishingly different from the storm raging in her life.

It was the time of my annual fast, when Bahá'ís abstain from food and drink from dawn to sundown each day. Bahá'u'lláh proclaimed the days of fasting between March 2 and 21 a period of grace, in which every hour is endowed with a special virtue while believers submit their wills to the will of God. I dedicated my effort to Naomi and thought about all the freedoms that had been taken from her since her illness had begun.

Soon the doctors ordered more scans to gauge the success of the transplant. Naomi was so frightened about what the big machines would reveal, that she begged me to sleep beside her the night before our return to the hospital. Knowing she had done everything asked of her and had fought hard for the right to live, I imagined her fright if the scans showed that the cancer remained. Submission to the unknown cut like a knife when Naomi's life was at stake—we were entirely vulnerable to being crushed. Side by side together in bed, we prayed for assistance, summoning God's protection and healing. Soon I could hear her sleeping and continued to pray alone.

The next morning, as I sat in the imaging waiting room and Naomi lay on the scanning table, I listened to the technician telling her to take a deep breath and hold it while the huge machine made rapid clicking noises and passed over her body. When the tests were over, we were promised results by that afternoon. Everyone was eager to know the outcome. Finally the doctors called and told us the scans looked good and that the nodules in the lungs had disappeared. The team of physicians, however, needed more time to assess results.

Meanwhile, my father had flown in from California to be with us. The next day, we met with Dr. Katz, who had recently joined the pediatric oncology team. He explained that the doctors wanted to give Naomi one last treatment, called spot radiation. The hospital in Dallas was one of the few places in the United States doing this procedure, which involved complicated mathematics, advanced equipment, and pinpoint accuracy.

Later that day, as Naomi and I were driving with my father to lunch, I was in a bitter mood, thinking to myself that Naomi had to endure one hardship after another without respite. "Please, Lord! Treat us special, just this once," I pleaded. Just then, I felt a sharp pain in the middle of my back and lurched forward with a yell. Turning my head, I saw a wasp fly out the window. My father and Naomi were as surprised as I that a wasp had materialized from nowhere and stung me in the car. Convinced the sting was a message, I asked myself what it could mean. Maybe, I thought, I am being reminded not to let weak thoughts get the upper hand over my deeper emotions. *Maybe spirit has visited with a strong reminder to stay on the warrior path.*

After my father returned home to Santa Barbara, Naomi and I stayed with David another two weeks while she received spot radiation treatments, spending most of our free time together visiting parks, producing artwork, watching movies, and socializing with David. During one of our visits to the hospital, Dr. Breva removed the catheter that had been dangling out of Naomi's chest for over a year. Symbolically, this event signified her freedom from devastating medical procedures and hope for a better future.

Following the completion of her treatments, we went back to the oncology unit for a last physical exam to see if she was ready to go home. While in the examining room, Naomi asked the doctor, "How's Jason? I e-mailed him but never got an answer."

Sadly, she was told that Jason had died of complications during his transplant. Another casualty. The news shocked Naomi, who for days recalled his strong words of encouragement to her. Several times over the next week, she mentioned how she missed him and did not want to believe he died. I remembered Jason's mother and thought how crushed she must be by the sudden turn of events, then I prayed for her and silently gave thanks for Naomi's continued healing.

At last we could go home and begin to put our lives together. After scheduling follow-up scans for June, we left the hospital; bid farewell to David, Ben, and Lori; and returned to Santa Fe to begin a new chapter.

On the flight home I was able to assemble my thoughts about our two-and-a-half-month stay in Dallas. Naomi, I realized, was helping me learn the code alluded to in my dream years before. At her lowest point, she said, "Thank you, God, for the opportunity I have been given." Despite finding herself in the darkness of this world, alone in the deep turbulent ocean with the shark of death nearby smelling her blood, she dealt with her fear by saying, "I know that my angels and God are going through this with me—I don't need to worry." Then I smiled, remembering that her favorite song was Bob Marley's "Three Little Birds," with the refrain, "Don't worry about a thing, because every little thing is gonna be all right."

Thinking back to the wasp in the car, I concluded that I was stung because I had strayed from learning the code. The wasp sting was spirit giving a reminder that life is unpredictable and will bite like a shark. A warrior neither complains in such situations, nor grieves over his circumstances; rather, he lets go and lives in the ocean of God's grace, trusting and fearless.

LIFE IS SO BEAUTIFUL

*My vision is the knight without armor, because he
is stronger without it.*

By mid-March, Naomi was physically weakened and bald, but her spirit was strong as she returned to school. Friends and teachers were touched to have her back.

The pictures for the upcoming yearbook were handed out, and Naomi's was startling. Not only was she bald, but her eyebrows and eyelashes were all but missing. Although I suggested substituting a picture from an earlier time, she looked wistfully at the photograph, and said, "Let it be. It's okay, because my friend Peggy and I are buying a page to share in the back—there will be other pictures of me there." While dismayed by the portrait, I nevertheless admired her strength, for someone else might have cried over such misfortune.

As the last days of high school approached and Naomi's graduation announcements were mailed off, friends and relatives sent their heartfelt congratulations. The prom was also drawing near, and as pairs formed for the big night, Naomi, determined not to miss anything, asked a young man she was friendly with to be her date. Chris, a top honors student and captain of the soccer team, readily accepted Naomi's invitation, and when she told us she had a date for the prom, we were incredulous at her pluck and good fortune, since she was still bald, and weak on her left side.

On prom night, Naomi dressed in a sleek black floor-length gown and stood in front of her bedroom mirror putting on makeup. She wrapped an elegant black silk scarf around her head, fastening it in front with a jeweled pin. Chris showed up, and I realized it was the first time I had experienced the pleasure of a young man arriving at my house to take out one of my daughters. My heart leapt with gladness to see standing in our entry, a very handsome and well-mannered teenager dressed in a tuxedo, with a corsage in hand for Naomi. She also had a corsage for Chris, and after they had pinned the flower arrangements on each other, I took pictures of them standing together. As Naomi turned to go, the weakness in her body caused her foot to twist in her high heel, and she fell down. It shocked us. But she was back on her feet in a flash, saying breathlessly that she was okay. Jean and I stood at the front door, watching as the couple drove away in the twilight, and we were moved by Naomi's determination to take advantage of every milestone in her life. As the car disappeared, Jean said, "She won't miss a beat."

On the day of graduation, Naomi put on her blue and gold cap and gown and left early to meet with the senior class. Jean, Sarah, and I drove across town to pick up Naomi's mother Kathleen and her brother Patrick for the ceremony. We arrived at the crowded outdoor stadium just in time to see the class walking out onto the green field. Soon Naomi appeared in a long line of students strolling toward their chairs in front of the stage, where the diplomas would be handed out. Glancing up at us in the bleachers, she smiled and waved. It was exhilarating to

Sarah with Naomi at graduation

see her happy among her peers, and we felt extremely proud of her accomplishment. After the principal, valedictorians, and guests finished their speeches, the seniors were called one by one to receive their diplomas. A cheer went up after each student's name was announced, but when Naomi's name was called, her classmates gave her an especially loud salute. We cried watching her clamber up the stairs and, smiling broadly, accept her diploma. Nobody knew as we did what she had achieved to be present at this moment. Only two months earlier, she had almost died when after ninety-six hours of continuous chemotherapy she was without an immune system.

At the end of the ceremony, the graduates hurled their caps into the air with great shouts of joy, and parents rushed onto the field to be with their children. Finally locating Naomi among a crowd of friends, we hugged her and gave her flowers. Seeing her cry from happiness, we knew time was a gift of inestimable value.

It was still June when we returned again to Dallas for more scans, after which the doctors said Naomi was doing "quite well" because the tests indicated a positive response to chemotherapy and radiation. It felt good to have the worst behind us now and to be able to look forward with faith to the future. Naomi wrote: "The cancer that was once a part of my body physically, but never mentally, is now gone forever. I see clear lungs, a healthy, cancer-free body, and a strong runner finishing a race in first place. God, I am thankful for life, and the gifts of healing you have showered on me."

During the summer, Naomi accepted both a part-time job in a gallery and part-time work in a clothing store. The gallery owner, who had at one time been my gallery director, knew what an enthusiastic and trustworthy worker Naomi was. He liked her readiness to apply herself, despite her ordeal, and was delighted to hire her.

Having learned that her application to The Rhode Island School of Design had been rejected—an understandable outcome, since she had completed it during her bone marrow transplant—Naomi decided to apply to other art colleges, for which more examples of her work were needed. She painted in oils and studied figure drawing at the home of a local artist. The relaxed, informal atmosphere chased away tensions, and we sat next to each other, which made it easy for me to occasionally glance at her work and give pointers, or simply admire her sense of proportion and values of light and dark. At the end of each session, the artists mingled with one another for refreshments and conversation before leaving. Naomi's hair

Naomi's self-portrait
oil on board
July 1998

was still short, and most everyone knew from my earlier remarks that she had been struggling with a devastating cancer, so they were surprised when she joked, smiled, and engaged in easy conversation. I was happy sharing my artistic pursuits with her and seeing her included in the creative community. She enjoyed our adult time together as well, often remarking when we left, "That was fun!"

Another project she undertook that summer was making papier-mâché masks, something she had been introduced to in high school. Now she continued on her own, incorporating various materials such as earth, flower petals, straw, and gauze. Each face seemed to emerge as an expression of her soul: a flower fairy with a crown of rose petals one day, an ogre with a dirt-encrusted face and straw hair the next. She also worked beside me in my studio, painting a self-portrait that came to bear a striking resemblance to her. It was painstaking work, and she groaned loudly, gazing for hours at her features. I knew from experience how painting a self-portrait can bring submerged feelings about oneself to the surface. At every moment, you are mirrored back at yourself, and it is easy to become exasperated because trying to create your own likeness on the canvas is difficult. For Naomi looking intently at herself, the signs of her chemotherapy ordeal were quite evident, and her hair was only a thick fuzz on her head. I offered pointers and critiqued her work until at last she had finished. To her credit, she had not only made a good likeness but also showed the talent an art college seeks.

Her stamina and zest for life continued to be amazing. Jean's parents had been giving the girls money each year toward college tuitions, and in July, Naomi used some of her money to buy a new Toyota Corolla sedan. But more than anything else, being with other people made her happy, and her appetite for living may have been the medicine that was saving her. Also, she had created a simple visualization for herself, written on a piece of paper and shoved into the drawer of her desk at home—a warm and beautiful picture of her future: "I have a family, and we work together on the farm. I am joyful being alive. I smell the fresh air, the soil. We have a nice little house, and we don't need a lot of money. God is important. I grow old, and walk around the land every day. I die peacefully."

About this time, one of our neighbors found out she had lymphoma. It was especially surprising because she, her husband, and two sons loved outdoor activity, and she had won tournaments at a local tennis club. Our neighbor had supported Naomi and now Naomi went to her, toting the journal she had kept during her treatments, and a blank journal for this woman to write in. On the last page of Naomi's journal she had written, "The doctors said that the scans look good. *No signs of it left!*" Just below this she added, "I am going to lend this diary to my friend to help her get through what I just did. I know she will be okay."

In mid-August we left for a two-week vacation to visit friends in Wrightsville Beach on the North Carolina coast. Unbeknownst to us, Hurricane Bonnie was brewing over the Atlantic Ocean and was starting on a course that would take it directly through our destination. Soon after we arrived, police evacuated the population of Wrightsville Beach, so we helped board up our friends' home and left for Wilmington, about a half-hour drive inland, where we checked into a motel. Minutes later, the hurricane rolled directly over us. We watched, fascinated as rain flew horizontally and 130-mile-per-hour winds bent trees, sometimes uprooting them altogether. The electricity went off, and at bedtime Naomi read to Sarah by candlelight. The next day, we drove to catch the ferry for Bald Head Island, a pristine area of dunes and beaches off the North Carolina coast. We were among the first to set foot on the eerily quiet island after its closure during the storm. The house we rented stood only a few hundred steps from the ocean, and the island was almost empty, inviting a luxurious privacy. The girls spent hours on end frolicking in the ocean, bodysurfing waves onto the shore and then going into deeper water to catch the next one, all the while shouting with glee. Naomi called it the best vacation of her lifetime. I wondered how fate had placed us in the midst of a hurricane when our lives were in such tumult.

After our unusual vacation, it was time for us to return to Dallas for follow-up tests. One evening Naomi came home from work visibly upset. In tears, she said she was afraid the tests were going to show that the cancer had come back. Anxious ourselves, Jean and I nonetheless tried to calm her, assuring her of how well she had been doing so far. She had tasted life as it could be—was meant to be—but if in Dallas the scans turned up something unexpected, it could ruin the hopes she had expressed for "miles of life ahead."

I flashed on a conversation I'd had with Naomi when she was ten years old. She had complained that something frightful was following her and she was scared. I told her, "Imagine yourself turning around and facing whatever it is."

But now, as I tried to calm Naomi's fears, I could not follow this advice, for my own fear was kindled. I could not face the prospect that her intuition might be true, because I was frozen by the unthinkable and could not turn around to possibly see death taking her.

THE MAELSTROM

*It scares me sometimes how powerless I feel
at the most powerful opportunities.*

The first week of September, Naomi and I flew to Dallas, where we rented a car and drove to David's house. That night, Naomi was so apprehensive about the next day's scans that she asked if we could sleep together in the guest room's queen-size bed. I knew she was entirely vulnerable and needed my strength to help fend off the demons of darkness coming to test her while she lay alone in the dark. We got under the covers together, hugged, and said prayers. Then she fell asleep.

The next day we first went to Dr. Gerhardt's office for scheduling, and then to the Pediatric Oncology Unit at the hospital to get a physical exam. Everyone was upbeat about how well Naomi looked and how positive she was. When Dr. Breva felt the former site of the hip tumor, Naomi squirmed and said, "That tickles!" Dr. Breva smiled and replied, "You feel fine."

Finally we went for the exams—a CT of the lungs and MRI of the pelvis—which Naomi abhorred because she did not like being in the cold, dark examining rooms, strapped into huge machines that were looking for signs of cancer. I waited in an adjacent room, listening anxiously to the familiar clicking noises of the scanning devices, and I prayed for God to protect her.

The following morning we drove back to Dr. Gerhardt's office for the results. In the waiting room was a woman with her sick, wheelchair-bound daughter holding a coloring book on her lap. The girl was about seven years old, and her left leg had been amputated at the knee. She looked pallid and weak, with barely any hair left from chemotherapy. Across the room was a boy about nine years old with his father. Watching him glance nervously at the girl missing her leg, I wondered if he feared that someday he, too, would be missing a leg. Within moments, Naomi instinctively went over to the girl, bent down next to her, smiled, and asked politely what she was doing. The child's face lit up, and as she shared her coloring book and crayons, the two chatted and drew together until Naomi's name was called. Then a nurse took us to an examining room: a tiny white cubicle with a window, one chair, a medicine cabinet, an examining table, and a light box on the wall for viewing X rays. There we made small talk and fidgeted, all the while becoming increasingly anxious and annoyed at the interminable wait for Dr. Gerhardt. After what seemed an endless interval, he showed up and summoned us into a larger room with a far more sophisticated light screen, where a track moved the cross-cut images sequentially in front of his experienced eyes. Dr. Gerhardt, though cordial, was strictly analytical, and at last he told us, "It appears the cancer has returned to her hip in a different place and probably the lungs, although we are not certain at this point."

My heart sank. "Are you certain? Perhaps there is some mistake," I asked anxiously.

"No, my radiologist is quite reliable. There is no mistake," he assured us.

The world seemed to suddenly collapse, as if we were in a maelstrom spiraling into a dark abyss of hopelessness. It was the worst moment of the entire ordeal, because our options were so reduced and because Naomi had struggled with every ounce of her strength to regain her life only to feel it all crumbling with the words "it is back." Dr. Gerhardt matter-of-factly dictated his analysis for the record into a microphone and then ordered a biopsy of the growth on her hip. Still in shock, we were escorted first to a nurses' station to get instructions for the biopsy and then to a secretary to pay our bill. A few minutes later we were sitting frozen and speechless in the car. Naomi was badly wounded, *as if an arrow had been driven deep into her heart*. Stunned and bewildered, I barely felt strong enough to drive.

The biopsy was scheduled for late in the afternoon, so we headed back to David's house, stopping along the way to pick up food for lunch although neither of us was hungry. When I told David about our visit with Dr. Gerhardt, he was speechless, and although it was evident that he wanted to say something to cheer us up, the gloom was too heavy.

Since it was hot, Naomi and I put on our swimsuits and went to the pool. After swimming for a while, she threw tennis balls into the water for the dogs to retrieve. She remained silent, no doubt processing her options and gathering fortitude for what now seemed an impossible struggle.

We arrived for the biopsy dazed and tired. Sitting in the hallway, Naomi took my hand and, while glaring straight into my eyes as if to say, "I hate this!" wrung it so hard I thought the bones would break. Then I knew that underneath her otherwise calm exterior there raged a storm that could barely be contained. I felt her hurt deeply, and I struggled to remain composed. Faced with similar setbacks before, I had relied on faith, prayed for healing, and trusted. Now I was numb with disbelief.

At last we were called for the biopsy, and Naomi was put on a table under a scanner. The doctor anesthetized the site with several injections before using the much larger biopsy needle, which he guided into the tumor while watching a screen that showed its path through tissue. As if wanting me to feel the agony and pain, Naomi squeezed my hand tightly, angrily digging her nails into my skin until I bled. I nervously joked about the grip on my hand. Then after the sample had been collected, we left.

Although the team of doctors at the Pediatric Oncology Unit had not seen the scans, and the biopsy results were not known, it felt like we had come to the end of our treatments in Dallas, so we decided to return to Santa Fe on our scheduled flight the next day. That evening, David and Ben took us out with their girlfriends to dinner at Morton's, a fancy Dallas restaurant. There Naomi ate politely and smiled occasionally during the conversation. The next morning, David drove us to the airport and we boarded our flight to New Mexico.

On the plane we were somber and silent. I tried to rest but felt as though I was being sucked down into quicksand. Anxiety and sorrow gripped me, even though I tried to be outwardly composed. Not only was I sad about Naomi's condition and our dwindling options, but also and worse, I questioned the faith that had been my strength and that I had relied upon. I felt bewildered about what I had been believing, including prayers and thanks I had been giving God for healing Naomi. What was His plan for us—hardship without relief, and then death? My confusion momentarily lifted on our descent into Albuquerque, and a voice inside me said, *"Learning the code requires complete surrender. It is made difficult on purpose—like gold that is tested for purity by being cast into fire."*

After landing, Naomi remembered that her good friend Alexis was in Albuquerque at the state fair that weekend, showing her livestock. We drove to the fairgrounds to search for her. As we walked through the crowds, Naomi asked what I was thinking, and I said, "I am struggling to understand what is happening now, because it seemed that everything was going so well. I have been trusting in your recovery, giving thanks, and now there is this setback . . . which confuses me. My faith has been shaken."

"I know," said Naomi, processing her own disappointment.

I could not tell her how devastated I felt coping with something so big it caused my inner logic to crash. My beloved daughter was facing a cruel and painful future, and I could not bear it. Every time the thought of her dying came to mind, I was flooded with intense consternation and panic.

We wandered over to the livestock exhibit where Alex was to be showing her goats but could not find her. After inquiring and searching for another forty-five minutes, we gave up and left. It had been disconcerting and odd walking around the fairgrounds amidst happy, festive crowds, while mulling over our fate. I almost wondered why everyone was carefree and jovial with death so near.

About halfway home, frustration and remorse at last overcame Naomi. She burst into tears and wailed that she had done everything expected of her, had given more than 100 percent, and didn't know what else she was supposed to do. She sobbed while we drove through the barren desert landscape. Then as ghostly clouds drifted casually across the bright blue sky overhead, casting immense shadows over the earth, she screamed, "I don't want to die of cancer! I might as well kill myself!"

Despite my own anguish, I tried to soothe her by sounding positive, telling her, "We still have possibilities. There are no closed doors in the universe."

Tired and lost in our own thoughts, we drove the rest of the way in silence, reaching home a little past noon. As we got out of the car, I walked over to Naomi and held her. Searching for something encouraging to say, it occurred to me that although her cancer had returned, it was much smaller than it once had been. I told her the cancer was not very large and that we would handle it. I had already begun thinking of alternative treatments, such as a fast, mineral wraps at a nearby healing spa, and a visit to a medicine man I knew on the Pine Ridge Sioux Indian Reservation in South Dakota.

Although our family was about to be gathered together again, which usually was time for rejoicing, a profound sadness pervaded our arrival. Naomi's life was in turmoil and her future uncertain. I opened the front door and announced we were home. Sarah was at school, but Jean came into the hallway and hugged Naomi, who stepped aside and went straight to her room. Jean wanted to discuss what had happened in Dallas, to get clear on matters, but Naomi was sullen and withdrawn, saying, "I don't want to talk."

Soon afterward, I asked Naomi to come join Jean in the living room, but she steadfastly refused. Trying to comfort Jean, I said, "You can't expect anything from her right now. She needs her space."

A half hour later, Naomi appeared from her room with a bundle of clothes under her arm, announcing, "I have to go to work now." As she was about to get into her car, Jean approached her in the driveway in front of the house and expressed surprise that she was leaving at 2:00 P.M., then asked, "Aren't you supposed to start work at four o'clock?"

Naomi gazed blankly at Jean and, opening her car door, said quietly, "No, I have to leave now . . . to get there early."

I too thought it odd to see Naomi clutching her little bundle of clothes and wanting to leave so hurriedly, but under the circumstances I decided to simply support her. We said good-bye, and Jean gave her a hug, whispering, "I love you!" As Naomi disappeared from view, Jean and I stood in the driveway with our arms around each other, determined to weather the storm that was wreaking havoc on our lives.

Usually when Naomi went to the clothing store late in the afternoon, she did not return home until after 10:30 P.M. That evening I fell asleep early and, waking up around 4:00 A.M., went to check on Naomi. Peering into her dark room, I could not make out her form under the blankets. Stepping closer, I discovered that the bed was empty. Although somewhat alarmed, I figured she had gone to a friend's house after work. Perhaps she had decided to spend the night, and did not want to wake us by phoning—or could not reach us because our phone was off the hook, as it often was at bedtime.

Around 7:30 A.M., I told Jean that Naomi had not come home

from work last night. Astonished, she checked to see if Naomi had left a message on our voice mail, which indeed she had, but to our surprise and dismay, all she said was, "Hi, everyone! Just wanted to let you know I am in Flagstaff, Arizona. Love you." Aghast and confused, I was glad at least to hear her voice sounded strong. She was heading west, and I guessed that she might drive to Santa Barbara, California, where my parents and her good friend Emma Brode lived. Nevertheless, we were concerned since she had left without any belongings, and we didn't know if she had money for essentials.

Immediately we phoned my parents, who were as incredulous as we were. My father suggested we wait a while for her to call again, and that she might show up in Santa Barbara, but in the meantime, that we find her license plate number in case we had to call the state police. Waiting nervously for Naomi's next call, I worried that she would run out of money, and thought of my precious teenager out on the road alone, in despair, stricken with cancer, and without even a change of clothing.

All that day we did not hear from her, nor did my parents. Unable to work, I spent most of my time either praying or doing little tasks around the house. That evening we still did not hear from her.

Then the next day around noon, my father called and said, "She's here, and we will have her call you soon." Within an hour Naomi phoned, sounding strong yet somewhat distant. We promised to send money and clothes. Hanging up, we realized she was on the next leg of her journey, and knew that now we had to let her forge her destiny alone. We were hurt that she had left so abruptly but glad for her safety.

SANTA BARBARA

The yearning in my heart to live is stronger than ever.

Naomi soon settled in to life in Santa Barbara, occupying a guest cottage at my parents' house, a single-story, corner-lot home in a well-established middle-class neighborhood. Trained as a sociologist, my father has had a varied career, ranging from work in the Kennedy administration with Robert Kennedy to director of the Field Foundation in New York City. An activist for progressive causes, including the containment of nuclear weapons, he was working alone as a consultant out of a small office in downtown Santa Barbara when Naomi arrived. My mother is more reclusive, usually staying home to paint or to read books on a wide range of subjects, especially science and psychology. Although forthright and honest about her feelings, she was unprepared for the tempest of emotion that almost immediately poured forth from Naomi.

While my mother prides herself on her toughness, she recoiled as Naomi vented her frustration, anger, and grief. The chaos that she had been fighting to control seemed to possess her very soul. She screamed and cried, throwing things about in a rage. She wondered why she had been born, and why she was helpless and so severely afflicted. Desperate to exercise control over her life and not be beaten by the cancer, she even mentioned suicide. My mother, helpless before this catastrophic outburst, withdrew, saying she was not a psychology professional and could not deal with Naomi's condition. My father made efforts to maintain composure, patiently expressing his sympathy and compassion from a distance. I heard what was happening from my mother, and although miles away, I knew Naomi was in catharsis. A feverish delirium beset her soul as she faced death, but she was not giving up.

Three days later, the worst of the storm had passed. After Naomi received a package from home containing her laptop computer and some clothes, she e-mailed Jean the following letter:

Dear Jean,

Thank you for sending my stuff in a jiffy.

I just want you to know I love you very much and that it is not your fault that I left, so don't blame yourself. I left because I was overwhelmed. I had the intention of killing myself because I did not want to suffer and die a slow death. I had the idea that I would overdose on a medication right before driving off a cliff, or jump off a waterfall, or swim out into the ocean at night and drown. These were my plans, but I did not follow through. Do you know why? I did not do any of those things because I feel the amazing love all around me. I feel life, and the yearning in my heart to live is stronger than ever before because of my experience. It might have been God's gift to me—to show me and give me the opportunity to really think.

I just wanted to share that with you.

Love,

> *Naomi*

Jean, deeply touched by Naomi's honesty, remarked, "Hearing about Naomi's desire to kill herself is saddening, but now I remember going outside to give her a hug and tell her I love her before she drove away. Knowing that people's love for her is what brought her back into the desire to live, I am so thankful I shared that moment with her."

Naomi's friend Emma was the first person she had contacted when she arrived. The Brodes had been friends of our family for many years. Originally from Santa Barbara, they met me soon after they moved to Santa Fe with their two young daughters, Emma and Carrie. My marriage to Kathleen had recently ended, and I was taking care of Naomi by myself. She was about to enter kindergarten, and Ann Brode suggested the Waldorf school, where Emma had been enrolled. Emma and Naomi became playmates, and for six months, Naomi lived with the Brodes when I needed time alone. I had become exhausted dealing with Kathleen's mental illness, running my landscape business, and single parenting. One of my first dates with Jean was for dinner at their home.

Eventually the Brodes moved back to Santa Barbara, but not before buying some land and a little house outside of Santa Fe. Because they continued to spend time in New Mexico each year, Naomi and Emma remained good friends.

Ann was well established in the healing arts community in Santa Barbara, with a steady massage practice. Soon after Naomi's arrival, Ann formed a small network of health-care practitioners to focus together on Naomi's healing.

Meanwhile, remembering how solidly vitamin B-17 had figured earlier in my meditations and how I did not know how to get it, instead finding B-12, I explored the Internet and found an organization called World without Cancer. Based in Florida, World without Cancer was closely affiliated with the Oasis of Hope hospital in Tijuana, Mexico, founded and run by world-famous cancer specialist Dr. Luis Contreras. Their premise was that cancer is a metabolic disease best treated by agents that influence chemical changes occuring in the body's cells. The main facet of the program was the intake of amygdalin, also known as laetrile or B-17. This agent, found in high concentrations in seeds and especially apricot pits, was said to destroy cancer cells by releasing traces of cyanide, which cancer cells absorb and healthy cells resist. Impressed by both the testimonials and the research, I called World without Cancer, and spoke with a staff member who further explained that while vitamin B-17 was the basis of the therapy, it was supported by shark cartilage to inhibit tumor growth, various other vitamins, and green barley powder, each of which had proved effective in fighting cancer and assisting health. I remembered a friend who had been diagnosed with ovarian cancer and received successful treatments in Mexico. While she was pregnant, a huge tumor was discovered in her uterus. The doctors were about to abort her fetus to begin chemotherapy when she felt impelled to save her baby. She left the hospital and fled to Mexico to seek treatment. There she was treated with laetrile, put on a special diet, and eventually brought her baby to full term, delivering a healthy girl; the remains of her tumor came out with the placenta. As a result of my friend's experience, I felt more encouraged about the possibility of laetrile and was eager for Naomi to begin treatment.

The group of healers in Santa Barbara who were focusing on Naomi, became the basis of The Healing Center Foundation. They were health practitioners devoted to healing through teamwork, group communication, and a combination of their different practices. Essentially, Ann Brode conceived the idea of the foundation after introducing Naomi to its cast of characters. Tony Allina, MD, linked her to the traditional medical world and introduced her to relaxation techniques and mind-body imagery. Naturopathic Doctor Luc Maes offered homeopathic and nutritional treatment. Herb Gravitz, PhD, provided psychological support, and Qigong master Chiyen Wong instructed Naomi in energy work and movement meditation.

I continued to ardently promote the laetrile program to Ann and encouraged Naomi also. Meanwhile, I learned that the B-17 was processed in Mexico at laboratories under strict quality controls and that tons of organic apricot pits from the US were continually shipped there to extract the oil.

Jean made phone calls to find out if there were unexplored opportunities for treatment within the mainstream medical community. The most promising possibility she discovered were clinical trials being conducted on Ewing's sarcoma patients at the National Cancer Institute, testing a vaccine designed to bolster the immune system's ability to fight cancer. The initial success rates looked good, and if Naomi's immune system was strong enough and if her genes carried a particular protein, she would be accepted into the program. The genetic protein would be extracted from Naomi and, with a substance called interleuken, would be recombined with her cancer cells, stimulating killer-cell activity against the cancer cells.

One day a doctor from the National Institute of Health (NIH) called our home to discuss details of the program, and I told him about my dream depicting doctors who were extracting cancer material from a patient's body, mixing it with protein, and reintroducing it. The doctor remarked with fascination, "That is it exactly!" This confirmation of an inner experience bolstered my spirits.

I prayed for guidance on whether Naomi should pursue the laetrile program, and continue to work with the healing team in Santa Barbara, or seek admission to the vaccine program. It seemed the laetrile, reported to be nontoxic, would act somewhat like the vaccine and would metabolically kill the cancer cells. Also, Naomi had developed strong ties with the healing community in Santa Barbara. Pursuing the experimental vaccine therapy would require moving to Washington, DC, where she knew only my brother Wade. So after considering the options, she remained in Santa Barbara.

Ann, picking up on my enthusiasm, also supported the idea of Naomi trying the laetrile treatment, saying it was great I felt so positive about it. When I called to order the products, the man asked who was going to administer the intravenous treatment. It had been his experience that because laetrile was banned in the US, people ordered it but could not find anyone to administer it. I thought Ann could find someone to help, but this proved more difficult than anticipated. Eventually, Dr. Allina agreed to oversee the placement of a line in Naomi's arm for infusions. Typically patients received two vials a day of the substance, but after faxing the Dallas doctors' medical reports to the physicians at the Oasis of Hope hospital in Mexico, we received a recommendation that the dosage be increased to three vials a day for twenty-one consecutive days. In addition, Naomi would take shark cartilage, other vitamins, and additional supplements, and she would begin a vegetarian diet to increase the effectiveness of the prescribed substances.

Dr. Allina arranged for a visiting nurse service to assist with the initial administering of the laetrile. Naomi e-mailed us that when the laetrile was first given, the smell of apricots was so strong that she and the nurse had joked about attracting fruit flies. For the first few days, the nurse helped fill the needle and insert it into her line, but soon Naomi was doing it herself. Following the recommended protocol, she also gave herself the shark cartilage suppository, took the additional vitamins and supplements, and changed to a vegetarian diet.

Naomi continued to establish herself in Santa Barbara, eagerly taking on a new life in an effort to unlock the door to a more promising future. She described powerful sessions with Chiyen, such as when sitting face-to-face and knee-to-knee with Chiyen, the energy which was sent through her hip and leg moved so strongly that she cried. The other practitioners also were having an effect, which bolstered our hopes. Knowing how reengaged Naomi was in her quest for healing, fullness, and certitude, I felt renewed confidence in her recovery. Moreover, from her E-mails alone I could tell she was coming into her own and was learning the code, gaining wisdom, and standing tall in the eyes of those who knew her.

12

DEEP WATERS

**I want to experience independence and be able to feel love
under all conditions.**

*E*arnest about pursuing her goals and dreams, Naomi sent in her updated portfolio and applications to colleges. Both the Art Institute of Chicago and the California College of Arts and Crafts, in Oakland, expressed interest in her. Finally deciding to concentrate on the school in Oakland, Naomi completed her entry requirement, including the following letter describing her background and interest in art:

> *The major influences in my decision to pursue fine art and design began when I was very young and will continue throughout my life. Art has been a way to express my emotions. I make art where some people write.*

One of my first influential memories was the smell of turpentine and paints. I remember sitting on my father's lap (an artist), with the clutter of discarded oil-covered rags on the floor around us. It was a dimly lit room with an old Victorian rose-patterned carpet. The tips of his brushes would often tickle my cheek as he applied color to the canvas in front of us.

In my elementary years I went to the Santa Fe Waldorf School, a school that focuses on the use of the arts to teach the child everything from language, math, science, and history, to music and bodily coordination. In this way we could see a whole picture of ourselves, helping to create a well-rounded person.

I was always the one who classmates approached to get drawings done. They would sneak their main lesson books (originally blank notebooks) over to my desk, where I would roughly sketch an outline of a person or a scene.

We live in Santa Fe, one of the top five places that people mark as a destination when looking for art. I have many memories of going to art openings and visiting galleries, admiring and noting the many techniques and styles. Nature in the Santa Fe area has also been a large part of me. The acres of open space that touch the horizon, the mountains, the wildflowers, and the seasons contribute to my desire to capture their glow and radiance in art. There are many mediums that I admire and want to try out. My favorite is oil. The oil color, made of pigments and oil, has a smooth, buttery texture. It can give the artist either great satisfaction or frustration because of its versatility. With its main characteristics of being used on large or small canvases, thinly or thickly applied, translucent or opaque, it dries slowly, thus allowing the artist to express himself or herself.

In high school my love of art grew and broadened. I had the most influential art teacher that I have ever had, besides my father who has been an ever-present figure in my world of art. In high school the concepts of negative space, positive space, rhythm, movement, repetition, and form played a major role in developing my art.

Today I am constantly exploring the great masters of other centuries, finding and learning new techniques that have been used for many years. Two of my favorite artists at this point are Amedeo Modigliani and Toulouse-Lautrec. Their work has given me inspiration and ideas about how I may improve my own art.

I was lucky to have the opportunity to go to Germany with my German class. We traveled all over Germany, visiting art museums, old churches, monasteries and castles. Throughout this time I sketched the German countryside with its green rolling hills and the five or more storied, white and reddish-orange tiled houses nestled in and around the dark green hills. The art of Albrecht Dürer and the golden, baroque styles of architecture gave me a sense of art history.

As I have said, there have been many influences leading me into the world of art. Undoubtedly, my father as an artist played the most important role. Also, the art of Santa Fe, my art teacher in high school, the Waldorf School, art books, my travels, and nature itself have all played major parts in my decision to pursue art and design, and in so doing, immerse myself in art for the rest of my life.

The California College of Arts and Crafts (CCAC) liked her letter and portfolio and asked Naomi to come for an interview. My father accompanied her to the Bay Area, where together they visited the college campus in Oakland. During her interview Naomi, with an intravenous line taped to her wrist and hair boyishly short, spoke about her background in art, also bravely mentioning her battle with cancer. The visit went well, and the counselor remarked that Naomi would be a good fit at the college.

Shortly after Naomi's return to Santa Barbara, our telephone rang, and a woman calling from CCAC asked to speak with Naomi, saying, "I would like to tell her that she has been accepted for admittance." I was elated, and when I gave Naomi the news that afternoon, she paused, hardly believing her success, then said, "Oh, wow! Really?" Immediately she sent in her deposit, eager to begin in the fall. We were all proud of her accomplishment, despite a bittersweetness due to the uncertainty about her future.

Meanwhile, my mother was alarmed at the laetrile Naomi gave herself each day—the vials clearly indicated their cyanide content.

This, combined with my mother's recent abdominal surgery and stress over other matters, caused her blood pressure to climb.

A woman who vigorously defends her way of life, she let her discomfort be known, and as a result it became increasingly difficult for Naomi to continue living in the cottage. Then one evening my mother called and asked to speak with me. With a serious tone to her voice and typical bluntness, she said Naomi did not look well, was weak, had brittle nails, and was being poisoned by the laetrile. Although I reminded her that chemotherapy was far worse, changes were to be expected, and no one ever died from taking laetrile, she remained adamant, insisting, "She is dying, Steven. Your daughter is dying!" I hung up furious at hearing those words, and then escaped to the dark fields outside. A terrible anguish gnawed at my heart, and as I prayed alone in the night, I cried. Shortly thereafter, to relieve the strain on my mother, Ann offered to let Naomi live in a spare room at her home.

According to Ann, when Naomi joined the Brode family, it became more closely knit. Ann, suspecting Naomi might indeed be dying, felt her house fill with a sacred peace, "a rarefied, supernatural feeling, as if the whole structure had risen to the heavens to be blessed by angels." As part of the family, Naomi performed chores, shared meals, and participated in activities. Ann and her husband Ben tried to give her the same opportunities as their own children and provide her with healthy diversions. Because Emma had a gasoline credit card, Naomi was given one too. When Ben joined a painting class at the city college, they encouraged Naomi to sign up also. Ann even proposed a Valentine's Day father-daughter art show—featuring work by Naomi and me along with art by Ben and Emma—to raise funds for Naomi's treatments, most of which were no longer covered by our insurance policy.

In early November, Naomi came back to Santa Fe for Sarah's twelfth birthday. She looked good, despite a yellowish cast to her skin from the laetrile. Her weight was around the usual 110 pounds, her hair, which had been straight blonde before the treatments, was now wavy brown and growing out, and she was relaxed except that she wanted to return to Santa Barbara as soon as possible to continue her work with the healers.

While she was home, she finished her last dose of intravenous laetrile and wanted to have the line removed from her arm. I remembered that the previous line inserted in Dallas had been removed while she was an outpatient, so I asked a registered nurse friend of mine if he could take this one out. He said that he thought so but needed to research it more. When I saw him next, he said, "The line goes all the way to her heart, but I spoke with a doctor, and I feel certain I can take it out." When he came to our house, I stood with him and Naomi in the bathroom as he slowly began pulling the long thin line from her vein. Naomi took deep breaths as more and more of the line emerged, repeating several times a Bahá'í prayer she knew from childhood: "Oh God, guide me, protect me, illumine the lamp of my heart, and make me a brilliant star! Thou art the Mighty and the Powerful!"[1] When at last the entire line was out, Naomi sighed in relief, confiding, "I have said that prayer a thousand times."

Later she surveyed her childhood home and asked about the two pine trees she had planted as seedlings when she was eleven years old. I flashed on her digging the holes in our yard and tending the pines as they slowly grew. Then I remembered deciding to move them, when they were three feet high, to the entrance of our driveway, one on either side. Naomi hadn't liked the idea, but went along with it anyway. Watering the new transplants, however, posed a problem since the hoses could not reach that far. So I would fill a wheelbarrow with water, push it up the driveway, and moisten the roots by hand. In time, they resumed growing and I came to think they symbolized both of our lives. It seemed much of Naomi's life had to do with pairs, and the big events for her came in twos. But the trees, now about four feet high, were getting brown needles. I had been preoccupied with Naomi and it had been a hot summer. The fall winds hastened evaporation. I tried, too late, to water more often, but it became clear that one of the trees was dying. Looking at Naomi with genuine remorse, I explained that one of the trees was not going to survive, and she said, obviously chagrined, "Dad, I told you not to move them. You didn't water them enough!" I explained how I would replace the dying tree, and then went out and bought another pine about the same height and planted it in the same spot, careful to ensure it established itself.

We rejoiced to have Naomi at home again, even for a short visit. Inwardly, I admired her strength and her ability to establish new friends and build a future on her own. When she returned to California, I could still feel her presence, and I prayed that God would help her overcome all her afflictions.

Now that Naomi's intravenous laetrile treatments were concluded, she had scans taken in Santa Barbara. They showed that the tumor on the hip was virtually unchanged, which Dr. Allina said was marvelous. The lung nodules, on the other hand, had increased slightly, but Naomi assured us this was because the healing team had been concentrating on the hip, and would now focus more on the lungs. She decided to continue with the laetrile protocol orally, as suggested, for an additional three months, along with the vitamin and mineral supplements and shark cartilage suppositories.

Meanwhile, although I tried to pursue a normal existence, inwardly I was constantly aware of Naomi's struggle and anxious about her healing. Sometimes I felt myself watching helplessly in the fading daylight as my valiantly struggling child, swept out to sea by the tide and alone with menacing sharks, strained to get back to shore. My thoughts kept returning to her in the deep waters.

Acutely aware that my faith was being tested, I began reading the biblical Book of Job, which described trials that felt similar to my own. Satan, knowing of God's love for Job, challenges Job's character, insinuating in front of God that it is only because life is going well for Job that he is grateful and faithful. Satan then wagers with God to let him ruin Job's life so that he loses faith. God agrees to let Satan test Job, with the condition that Job live. Consequently Job, whose faithfulness, uprightness, and hard work have been blessed with the bountiful rewards of earth and family, loses everything, including his children. Now destitute and in misery, with painful boils covering his body, he laments that he was ever born. Yet despite his bewilderment that a just God would subject him to such calamity, he remains faithful, saying:

> *Naked I came from my mother's womb, and naked shall I return; the Lord gave, and the Lord has taken away; blessed be the name of the Lord.* [2]

Reading these words and identifying fully with Job's helplessness and despair, I cried. At the same time, I realized that Naomi was teaching me compassion, for now my heart had come to know the unfairness of life—the terrible misfortunes that befall innocent people, causing them to either grow radiant in their faith or wall off their hearts out of bitterness.

For Christmas we planned to gather with Jean's relatives in Cincinnati for nine days. When we approached Naomi about joining us there, she hesitated, which surprised us, but eventually she agreed to come for five days. Once we had our dates figured, we made airline reservations and arranged for accommodations. We accepted an invitation to spend the first few days with Jean's brother Tom, his physician wife Barbara, and their children, Annie and Ben. They had extra room in their spacious house for our whole family. After that we planned to move to a guest house on the grounds of Jean's parents' high-rise apartment.

Jean, Sarah, and I arrived on December 22, a few hours before Naomi's flight was due to come in. I could barely keep my mind off her impending arrival as we ate dinner. Naomi had been a loving presence with Tom and Barb's kids during the times our families had gathered together, and when she fell ill, they had remained in close touch with her, especially through E-mail.

After dinner, Barbara and I headed back to the airport, talking along the way. Her father had died only a few years earlier from brain cancer, and she understood much of what we had been going through. Arriving at the airport, we were surprised to learn that Naomi's flight was early. We rushed to the gate, but when we got there, people were already deboarding. To our dismay, we did not see her. Then suddenly she appeared from behind us, smiling and looking relaxed, happy, and wonderful—nothing like the pale and weak person I had been imagining since my mother's comments about the terrible effect of the laetrile regimen. All the way home to Barbara's I thought, "Oh let this be true! Let this happiness last forever."

The Christmas Eve festivities were at Jean's uncle's home, where many relatives were overjoyed to see Naomi again. Frequently glancing her way, I was amazed at how beautiful she looked, smiling and graceful in her black sleeveless evening dress. I could scarcely believe my eyes and thought, could this happy vision last forever? Then the dark notion crossed my mind that in fact she was dying. Startled and angry, I protested with a loud "no," and prayed, "Please let her live, Lord!"

The days passed, and my happiness at being together again as a family continued to be eclipsed by fears about losing Naomi. Torn between faith and doubt, I began to worry that my own inner struggle would contribute to her defeat. As much as I wanted to be convinced of Naomi's healing, doubt remained.

Near the end of her trip, Naomi was caught off guard by a slight cold from the stress of travel and being in a cold climate with unfamiliar people. The evening before her return to Santa Barbara, my apprehension about her well-being was substantiated when, while packing, she looked up and said, "Dad, my leg has been hurting." Right away I sensed that she was really saying, "Dad, I have felt this pain before, and though I would like to believe it is some small thing, I fear it is not. I am doing whatever I can, but what if it is not enough?" To overcome the sinking feeling in my heart, I immediately tried to rationalize the symptoms, replying, "It is probably the cold, damp air you are not used to. It affects your leg." Naomi accepted this in silence—and no doubt with skepticism.

The next day Jean, Sarah, and I took her to the airport. She seemed weaker and more distracted than when she had arrived, which bothered me. I guessed that the trip had been taxing on her. After we all hugged and kissed, she vanished into the airplane. Jean cried, and we noticed too late that Naomi had left her jacket behind.

Back at Tom and Barbara's, we talked frequently about Naomi's condition. They were skeptical about the laetrile protocol but did not want to dash my hopes. At one point, Tom asked, "The doctors here in the States have families, and sometimes a member is stricken with cancer. If something could save that person, don't you think they would support it?" I could not answer him but thought that faith must play a part.

Soon after our return to Santa Fe, I called Ann Brode to see how things were going and to tell her how impressed I was with Naomi's progress. She explained that Naomi's pain was worse now, confirming misgivings she had had about Naomi's leaving on a long journey and being away from the healing team. She added that whereas before Naomi may have been winning, now it appeared that the cancer was gaining ground. Feeling as if I had been hit by a freight train, I asked, "But did her leg hurt before the trip?" Ann avoided the question, saying only that she was disappointed. Devastated, I hung up, thinking perhaps something had gone wrong during our time together, and that my doubts were being fulfilled. But neither Jean nor I could connect events over the brief Christmas vacation with the discouragement Ann had expressed.

My alarm and inner turmoil caused me to pray even more. I felt helpless beseeching the Almighty, not understanding why He did not give us more power to vanquish the enemy that plagued us. The root of my faith was that God is in everything, healthy cells and cancer cells, and that because He is limitless and holds dominion over all of creation, He would save us. Logically I thought, if something existed independent of God, even a single atom, it would mean that a power existed beyond Him, which would impose a limitation and prevent Him from being All-Powerful—an impossibility. No matter how bad events became, I clung to the belief that God could change them at any time and produce a miracle. Yet at the same time I began to reflect on all the terrible occurrences He permitted. I remembered that while Naomi was undergoing treatments in Dallas, a school shooting in Kentucky made headlines. Some high school girls had gone to school early to gather in prayer before classes, when a fourteen-year-old boy with a gun walked up to the group praying in a hall and proceeded to open fire. Eight students were hit, three of whom died from their wounds. This tragedy, witnessed by God as He listened to the young women's prayers, led me to believe that there is no protection offered to the living, that the world is a place of engagement and struggle—a proving ground for our spirit. Appropriately, Bahá'u'lláh wrote:

> O Son of Being!
> Bring thyself to account each day ere thou art summoned to a reckoning; for death unheralded, shall come upon thee and thou shalt be called to account for thy deeds. [3]

I had been seeing a psychologist named Arden Fisk. A short, trim man with a broad warm smile and attentive eyes, Arden listens very intently, as if living my experience with me. Now, while I talked about Naomi's battle and cried, I tried to make sense of her suffering in the context of faith in God. Arden listened compassionately as I struggled to maintain belief in Naomi's healing. Although I believed God protected her, I had an unconscious anxiety she was dying. As usual, Arden was careful not to direct me, but rather support my finding the truth through honest introspection. I could not accept that holding on tightly to hope for a miracle was denial of Naomi's circumstances. Faith is believing, I thought; how can we plan for the future if we don't believe a future exists?

THE ART OF LIVING

I am not ready to leave this world.

Naomi continued her treatments and other activities in Santa Barbara, describing some events in a card she made by hand and sent to Kathleen. On the front she drew in colored pencils an angel with a halo and wings, while inside she wrote in big letters, "An Angel Is Watching over You," and then related how she walked the neighbor's dogs, took trips to the beach, and enjoyed the beauty of Santa Barbara. Each Wednesday afternoon, the painting class took field trips. Naomi went with Ben, most often expressing herself in watercolors or oils. She also continued the intensive work with all her healers. By now she had finished taking the laetrile and was relying solely on their recommendations. The pain in her leg had become severe enough that painkillers had been prescribed—at first only light drugs like Vicodan, but then heavier medicines. Unfortunately, they caused nausea, leaving her with little appetite so that she began losing weight.

About this time, Naomi met Jill Martin, a professional photographer who liked taking pictures that explored the inner life of people. The daughter of a filmmaker, she had grown up in Los Angeles, was single, of medium height with short dark hair, and fair complexion with freckles. A client of Ann Brode's, Jill was drawn to Naomi from a photograph in Ann's office, and when the two were introduced, they hit it off immediately. One afternoon they went on a photo shoot among the hills along the beach. Naomi wore a black knee-length sleeveless dress, and was thin, with tomboyishly short hair. Jill held her Hasselblad camera at waist level and, while gazing into the viewer from above, snapped pictures of Naomi, arms outstretched and head thrown back, smiling, and a glorious look of openness and freedom on her face. Because of the upward tilt of the camera, Naomi seemed to be soaring, arms extended, above the dark hills behind her. This austere, beautifully haunting black-and-white series came to be known as the "Naomi flying" pictures.

The moment I saw them I remembered something Naomi had written when she was twelve:

> *I wish I could dream I was flying and feel how it felt. I always thought it would be neat, but I've never had a flying dream that I can remember! Maybe some day I will.*

In fact, her wings were now being tested for strength and endurance as she became an eagle learning to soar above the world of clay.

Naomi's circle of friends and supporters was expanding, while simultaneously she was coming to know herself remarkably well. As people were drawn into relationship with her, she honored their presence in her life as a precious gift, graciously shifting the focus of conversation from herself to them. Although sorely afflicted, she barely complained, even to her family.

Whenever we spoke on the phone, once or twice a week, I worried that my anxiousness would show. Life was not giving us

photo by Jill Martin

Naomi "flying"

any guarantees. However, despite our unspoken concerns, both Naomi and I remained positive during our conversations. We would not give in to fear, but looked to the future with hope.

As the Valentine's Day benefit art exhibit approached, Jean, Sarah, and I made arrangements to spend a week in Santa Barbara, and I sent out artwork in advance. Momentum for the show picked up significantly when the *Independent,* a Santa Barbara newspaper, printed a full-page article in the health section, headlined "Naomi Boone's Art of Living." It focused on Naomi's struggle with cancer and the group of healers who were assisting her. Early in the article, Naomi was quoted as saying, "I know people mean well, always asking me how I'm feeling and all that. But a lot of times they can't talk just about me. It's always about the cancer . . . I'd like to focus more on what I'm doing than on the fact that I have cancer." Later she acknowledged her helpers, explaining, "It's really unusual that a combination of so many different kinds of healers get together with just one purpose. But it's something that just feels right, like it's meant to happen this way. Here's this great group, they all have a different role to play, and yet they all work together." Dr. Allina spoke of the cancer and the team's efforts, noting, "Absolutely, the rate of progress (of the disease) has been much slower than would be expected without these treatments." Then he went on to say, "About Naomi's feeling of peace: We are not only trying to cure her of the cancer, but also trying to prepare her to die if we can't cure it."[1] The article also featured two photographs—a big one of Naomi wearing jeans and shirt, smiling, with her hands in her back pockets and her short hair tousled, and one of Ann and Dr. Gravitz in the garden outside their office building, where the exhibit was to be held.

As it turned out, my brother Brent and his girlfriend Angie had set their wedding date for the Saturday following the art show. This, too, was to take place in Santa Barbara, and I was asked to be Brent's best man, so we extended our travel plans.

Two days before the show, we arrived in Santa Barbara. The cottage behind my parents' house was ready for Jean and me, while Sarah would sleep at the Brodes' home with Naomi. The exhibit had been expanded to include the works of several local artists and my mother, an amateur painter of merit. Soon after we arrived, I visited my father at his downtown office and he showed me the article in the *Independent*. Although stunned by the remark that the healing team was "also trying to prepare her to die," I mentioned to my father I thought the article would be inspiring to many people struggling in life, for it showed Naomi's spirit and determination in the face of grim hardship.

Late that afternoon Naomi drove to the house. Parking along the curb beside the back gate, she got out of her car smiling, and we all exchanged hugs. After a lengthy time apart, we always greeted each other with much anticipation. I wanted to know that she was all right, and to support her, while she needed to feel normal and independent, yet assure us of her love.

The next day, Jean and I met Ann to preview the artwork. I was touched to see the walls filled with paintings contributed by various talented people. My paintings were hung along one wall, mostly monoprints—oil-based inks, painted and rolled onto a glass surface, then pressed onto paper. They included landscapes of Aspen trees blazing golden against a mauve sky, and cloud-filled sunsets glowing above darkening trees and land. Nearby hung three of Naomi's masks set in clear plexiglass boxes, and two of her small oil paintings of Northern New Mexico: a view of the Río Grande flowing through a gorge; and a panorama of sweeping plains backed by Pedernal, a striking mountain near the former home of the late painter, Georgia O'Keeffe. Naomi's paintings showed she was a promising young artist who exhibited both confidence in her brushwork and a subtle sense of color and light.

In a small area adjoining the main room, I saw Jill's photographs for the first time and was stunned. One in particular—four separate images of Naomi "flying," with arms outstretched and an exuberant, almost transfixed expression on her face, all mounted side by side within a mat in a single elegant frame—brought tears to my eyes, for it so perfectly captured her beautiful, young, free spirit. Hugging me, Ann said, "Jill wants your family to have any photograph at her cost." As we walked further around the room, stopping in front of a delicate landscape by Naomi, set in a gilded frame, Ann mentioned that we might want to keep it, in case Naomi died. Gripped by a sudden panic, as if giving voice to the prospect of Naomi's dying would hasten her demise, I had to compose myself and try to understand that there was indeed a medical point of view that Naomi's days were numbered.

When the doors opened to the public in the afternoon, about one hundred people strolled through the exhibit. It was then that Jean and I finally met the doctors and practitioners who were helping Naomi. Dr. Hodder, the pediatric oncologist, was a tall, dark-haired woman with a slight Australian accent. Dr. Allina, Naomi's general practice physician, proved to be very open-minded, and at ease discussing a wide range of subjects. Dr. Luc Maas, the holistic chiropractic physician, generated an abundance of earth energy; he was quick to smile and highly intelligent, and he spoke with an inflection from his native Belgium. The other two members of the healing team, Chiyen Wong and Dr. Herb Gravitz, were out of town, but we would meet them later.

Naomi arrived late, wearing a brown dress and sandals, accompanied by Emma and another friend, both in black sleeveless dresses and black platform shoes. I could tell Naomi felt uncomfortable being in the spotlight, especially since so much attention was on her battle with a devastating disease. Consequently, during the show she retreated to Ann's office with some friends and greeted smaller groups of visitors. Everyone, it seemed, was excited about the exhibit and its mission—enough so that despite being held in an off-beat location, it successfully raised money for Naomi's alternative treatments.

A few days later, I was invited to go painting with Naomi's art class, and eagerly welcomed the opportunity to be in a beautiful outdoor setting making art with her and other creative people. We set up easels next to each other along the shoreline and chose the same scene to render—a northwest view of the coast to where cliffs dotted with eucalyptus trees jutted out into the sea. Naomi had brought along a little square gessoed board, and I a larger rectangular canvas. Sarah, who had accompanied us, sat on a grassy area nearby, leaning against a palm tree and sketching with colored pencils. Caught up in the joy of creating art, our sense of time vanished, and before we knew it, the sun was casting long shadows behind us. As the air cooled, we decided to quit for the day. Naomi had done a splendid work: soft and muted, portraying the ocean spilling onto the shore, mountains in the background, and in the foreground, a palm tree waving in the breeze. My rendering of the scene was more pointillistic, with dabs of vibrant colors dancing over the surface of a red-primed canvas. Sarah's colored-pencil sketches were light and airy. The afternoon's immersion in colors, shapes, and nature's majestic harmonies, shared side by side with my daughters, had infused me with deep joy and gratitude. As we packed our materials, however, I noticed Naomi moving tentatively and slowly, and when we stopped at a health food market on our drive home, she lay curled up on the backseat. Even so, she looked up at me and remarked, "Wasn't that fun!" Unable to move because of a throbbing back pain, she reached for her medicine, telling Sarah and me to go shop. When we returned twenty-five minutes later, Naomi had gained control of her body again, and by the time we arrived at my parents' house for dinner, my sense of alarm had subsided.

Another day, while Naomi and I were driving to an appointment with her psychologist, she said something that made me realize she had been coming to terms with the gravity of her situation. "Everyone I have read about, and people I have met who have recovered from life-threatening illness, first had to accept their possible death." Touched that she had shared such an important insight with me, I began to realize that the work she had been doing with the healing team all these months had helped her reach a summit that offered a lofty view of her surroundings. It was a vantage point from which she could live even more powerfully.

My brother's wedding day approached, and everyone grew increasingly excited about the big event. Angie asked Naomi to be her bridesmaid, and Brent asked me to be his best man. We were fitted for tuxedos while Wade flew in from Washington, DC, and then my parents hosted a big dinner at their house for Angela's family and ours. After dinner as I was standing in the kitchen, Angie's grandmother touched my shoulder kindly and said that her entire family was praying for Naomi.

The wedding was held at a park high on a hill that overlooked the city. The sky was almost cloudless, and a slight breeze rippled through the otherwise mild air. A covered bandstand stood at one end of a grassy open space where chairs were set out. Soon, a long, white carpet was unrolled from the bandstand through the aisle between the chairs and up to an arch decorated with flowers in the middle of the field. Brent, Christopher, and I waited on the bandstand as the musicians played tender chords. Then Naomi, who was noticeably thin in her plum-colored short-sleeved silk dress, appeared under the arch, with a wreath of flowers on her head, and walked slowly and deliberately, step by step toward us. She held a bouquet in her hands and smiled bashfully yet proudly. When she reached the bandstand, she turned around and faced the entry, where Brittany appeared and stepped forward strewing petals. Finally, Angie, in her white wedding gown and holding her father's arm, came forward and joined us.

Turning to face the minister, we listened as she performed the marriage ceremony. When Brent had trouble placing the wedding ring on Angie's finger because his own hand was shaking badly, Naomi and I looked at each other. She winked, and then smiled. After the vows had been said and the guests had finished their refreshments, Naomi and Brent's best friend, Sam, tied cans to Angie's car and used cake frosting to write on the windows, "Just Married."

I felt happy for my brother and his new family. I also admired Naomi for participating while she was ill, making light of her pain and loss, laughing, turning outward with joy for others. From where I sat, Naomi's wings had certainly passed the test. They proved strong and enduring enough to lift her out of her personal anguish and keep her soaring through the festivities. Her wish for a flying dream, had it manifested as a dream, could not have been more thrilling than this very real, flesh-and-blood flight that was so exquisite for all to see.

The author with his two daughters at Brent's wedding

THE INVISIBLE BOND

*Show up and be lovingly present, no matter what it looks like
out there or inside yourself. Always speak the truth
of your heart.*

We returned to Santa Fe the day after Brent and Angie's wedding. Our visit had been good in many ways, and yet heartbreaking too, because Naomi was fighting a monster that gave her no rest. Increasingly, her many well-wishers asked, "How is she doing?" The most I could answer was, "She is strong, but cancer is a brutal disease. All we can do is trust in God."

More than ever I was sensitive to the suffering of innocents, and if in the morning newspaper I read an account of a child battling a terrible disease or killed in an accident, I wept. One morning an article on the front page leapt out at me. A teenager, cruising on a weekend evening in Española, a town north of Santa Fe, picked up two other teens who soon commandeered his car and drove him to a bridge near Taos, where they beat him and tried to throw him off. The drop, 1,200 feet into the Río Grande gorge, makes this the second highest suspension bridge in America. The lad struggled to hold on to the railing as the two hitchhikers continued to beat him and kick his hands until he fell to his death in the cold, raging river below. Then they stole his car and drove south to Mexico, where they were eventually apprehended. It made me angry that we were fighting for life with all our might, on our knees begging God for deliverance, while somewhere else, life for two teenage murderers had no worth and could be snuffed out without remorse.

This puzzling contradiction in values left me feeling confused and sad, thinking that perhaps if the two young men had ever truly known the beauty of life, they would not have seen it as easily expendable. Then I remembered words Naomi had written during chemotherapy treatments: "I love myself with all my might! I know that if I cherish myself first, before anyone else, then I heal. I am healing . . . I can feel it move through my body! Healing . . . loving . . . knowing . . . wishing . . . hoping . . . being . . . enjoying . . . living . . . mending . . . giving . . . praying . . . sending . . . shining . . . These gifts of life are what make it possible to fight so hard to keep it." Because I witnessed Naomi chasing her dreams with death on her heels, applying to colleges, and making efforts to remain positive in the midst of her pain, it was hard to understand why anyone would violate, or even fail to appreciate, the preciousness of life, much less hurt other people.

Jean, meanwhile, resumed contact with the NIH about the clinical trials using vaccine therapy. Naomi, feeling that she might be losing her battle, was ready to try this approach. Wade, who lived only five minutes from the NIH facilities, offered to let us stay with him during treatments. Consequently, I began making plans to live in Washington, where I had grown up. If all went as expected, we would arrive in spring, when cherry blossoms bloomed around the tidal basin at the Jefferson Memorial. Perhaps I would find a studio where I could paint.

Clearly, Naomi's condition was worsening. Her leg and back pain continued, and nausea disrupted her eating. Worse, she increasingly noticed that it was harder and more painful to move. In effect, she was slowly becoming paralyzed.

Feeling hemmed in, and in search of more comfort and support, she expressed her longings for her mother, writing in her journal:

Dear Mom,

I yearn for your smile, laugh, joy, and your glow. You are not always like that, though. I have seen you when you thought there were computers in your head and creatures following you. Those times were hard. I would worry about you when you got really skinny, when you were smoking constantly, when you were put into the hospital.

In the eighth grade I fainted when our class went to the hospital to learn about the human body. I feel like the reason I fainted was because of my emotional trauma from seeing you ill.

I yearn for a mother I don't really have, one who is always there.

I feel like running, but the only way I can do that is in my dreams.

We want to be healthy, strong, and reliable. Your presence, even though it can be embarrassing, is honored in my heart. I love you, Mom, and look forward to seeing you soon.

It is hard to tell you when I am hurting because then I worry that you will freak out . . .

Naomi realized that Kathleen had been weakened by long years of illness and that every child's birthright—a dependable mother who could be a springboard to the future—was not available to her. Yet she yearned for the magical, safe feeling of maternal protection and love that was embedded deep in her memory.

The miles of life that she had anticipated would unfold before her, were now like a mirage in the desert. Each day, her life was becoming more brutally constrained and painful. Cancer was turning upon her pitilessly.

One evening, Emma and Naomi went out together in Santa Barbara. Ann and Ben had established a curfew of 2:00 A.M., but the girls did not return until 4:00 A.M. As a result, a typical teen-versus-parent battle ensued over the curfew requirement, and Naomi finally stated, "If I am going to die anyway, what difference does it make?" Her reasoning was sound, because the exigencies of her life had become different from those around her; for Naomi, life was measured in moments rather than years.

Emma found her friend's pain and closeness to death deeply troubling. When she first learned of Naomi's illness, the mere thought that Naomi might not always be with her came as a shock, because for years the two had planned to attend college together and then after graduating, to live in the same town. Over time the shock turned to confusion about her own direction, and Emma stayed away from home more, engaging in activities on her own.

Naomi confided to my father one afternoon that she had wanted to do volunteer work but feared doing so because Jason, her friend from Dallas with leukemia, had done volunteer work when he was out of the hospital, and when he went back in he died. The association of volunteer work with death vexed her. Although she continually strove to maintain thoughts of a rosy future, the bony hand of death always seemed to wither the rose. Often now, whenever she felt exuberance an irrational fear would come over her that if she accomplished her desire, it might be the last thing she ever did in life. She wrote, "I made a list of things to do, and then thought, when I am done with the list I will die! I hate these thoughts that are coming up." Suspicions clouded her spirit, so that simply living was not simple at all.

About this time Naomi was having difficulty climbing stairs, including the steep flight of thirty steps or more to the front door of the Brodes' home. Consequently, arrangements were made for her to live in Brent and Angie's home, a single-story house with a tiny front lawn, located on a crowded block in a quiet, middle-class neighborhood. A small swimming pool took up almost the entire backyard, and the garage had been made into an office. Brittany gave up her bedroom and moved into Christopher's room, where they shared his bunk beds. With only five rooms in the house, the one bathroom in the hall by the kitchen had to accommodate all of them. In return for staying there, Naomi offered to drive the kids to school.

To apply to the NIH experimental cancer treatment program, candidates had to submit biopsies. But we learned Naomi's biopsies done in Dallas were now too old, so new ones were scheduled at Cottage Hospital in Santa Barbara. Feeling as though her options were running out, Naomi wanted to participate in the clinical trials as soon as possible. Incredibly, however, the first biopsy results from Santa Barbara were botched, and she had to repeat the uncomfortable procedure. A week later the more shocking news came back that she would *not* be accepted. She was among a small group of people with Ewing's sarcoma who lacked the genetic protein needed to produce the vaccine. I was incredulous, especially since I had trusted that my dream about reintroducing a healing substance into the body had been revealed for a purpose—that it was a helpful sign. Everyone was dismayed and didn't know what direction to pursue next. Furthermore, Naomi's pain was increasing, and she was becoming paralyzed . . . yet no one knew.

Three days after learning that Naomi was not accepted by the NIH, I got a surprise call from Brent, whose somber greeting alerted me that something was wrong. He told me that Naomi, extraordinarily upset by the NIH disappointment, had swallowed a bunch of pills and had gone to the ocean during the night to drown herself. By luck, a stranger had been on the beach, interfering with her plan.

I was stunned. Trying to grasp the reality of the almost unreal vision that had been presented to my mind, I asked, "Was she wet when she arrived at the house?"

Brent sadly went on to say, "Yes, she was wet. We took her to the hospital . . . She's okay now, but we were awake all night making her throw up."

With this unexpected turn of events, my hurt and fear turned to anger for not having been with Naomi at such a painful time. Was it luck or fate that seeing a stranger on the beach had reminded her of the invisible bond she shared with life and ultimately saved her? A wave of guilt passed through me. I asked Brent if I should come out, and he replied, "No, she is all right."

When I told Jean the news, she was, like me, stupefied. Naomi had long inspired us to believe that we would all overcome this horrible circumstance. As we wondered what was happening to her, a dark omen clouded our thoughts: *The arrow had sunk deeper, and the shark was a little closer now to its victim.* Feeling how maddening it was to be so far away, so powerless to help, I cried for my beloved daughter who had always expressed so much joy in life. Turning my gaze to heaven, I asked, "God, where is your helping hand?"

As the days passed, we resumed our search for a cancer treatment that would be a cure. It seemed my faith was being met with heartbreaking disappointment at each turn. The world's vanities had lost their allure, leaving emptiness. My soul searched for meaning, and I turned again to the Book of Job, feeling his trials like they were my own, as in passages such as the following:

> *Why is light given to a man whose way is hid, and whom God hath hedged in?*
>
> *For my sighing cometh before I eat, and my roarings are poured out like the waters.*
>
> *For the thing which I greatly feared is come upon me, and that which I was afraid of is come unto me.*
>
> *I was not in safety, neither had I rest, neither was I quiet; yet trouble came.* [1]

Over the course of Naomi's illness, I had been journeying with her through the valley of the shadow of death, holding tightly to prayer and faith for comfort. Arden Fisk knew the extent to which I relied on spirit and sacred texts in solving tests. Now during our sessions, I increasingly doubted my faith that we were being helped so that Naomi would survive. From the beginning, I had put my trust in the concourse of angels who were surely assisting us. Certainly, I felt, God's healing will be with Naomi, considering all the prayers on her behalf and her own tremendous will to live. I knew from the Bahá'í writings that God hears and answers prayer. Faith had been my greatest ally, an oasis in the desert; now it seemed illusive. Yet in my heart, I knew it had been so for others who had gone before us. My earlier immersion in the Book of Job had reminded me that God tests his loved ones. He casts them into the crucible—a struggle perhaps best symbolized by the crucifixion of Jesus. I concluded that I had to be stronger, keeping my faith in God's mercy no matter what, as God indicated to Job when He said:

> *Gird up thy loins now like a man: I will demand of thee, and declare thou unto me.* [2]

Job, I knew, accepted the challenge. When his wife, exhausted and angry at their constant, cruel misfortune, was surprised that he still maintianed his integrity, and then said to him, "Curse God and die," faithful Job replied, *"Shall we receive good at the hand of God and not evil?"* [3]

'Abdú'l-Bahá, the son of Bahá'u'lláh, also endured many heartbreaking tests, and by his Father's will, became the central figure of the Bahá'í Faith after Bahá'u'lláh's passing. This teacher, whom Bahá'ís adoringly refer to as the Master, said:

> *But regarding the tests: Undoubtedly they must be violent so that those souls who are weak may fall back, while the souls who are firm and sincere may shine forth from the horizon of the Most Great Guidance like unto sparkling stars.* [4]

Although I had come to these scriptures for my own fortitude, they helped me see that life itself had already forged a remarkable being in Naomi. Now, after another terrible blow had knocked her down, she picked herself up once again, even though her flame of hope was flickering out under the unrelenting assault of adversity.

THE LOGOS

As of now, I let go of my fears and troubles. In their place I let God do the work. I let light and energy, wholesomeness and happiness enter my soul. I know that everything will be all right because God is with me no matter what.

One night, before I was scheduled to see Arden the next day, I had a dream:

I was in a small room in an unfamiliar building, waiting for a doctor to arrive. It was well lit, with spare furnishings and two doorways, one leading outdoors and the other to a hall that went to other rooms. Dr. Levi appeared in the doorway, with information to share about Naomi. He told me that she was tired and needed medication, which I objected to, suggesting aspirin instead. "She needs to drink a bottle of soda pop each day," he added, beaming. Then he smiled and said, "I want to show you this." He handed me a piece of lined letter paper filled with Naomi's handwriting and urged me to notice the writing. The initial four or five sentences were in Naomi's characteristic script, but beginning with the next line, her writing was indecipherable. The letters seemed more like hieroglyphics—short little straight lines set together at angles, incrementally becoming darker and heavier, as if she had exerted greater pressure with each mark.

When I awoke, I was puzzled at both the handwriting and Dr. Levi's jovial mood. It seemed that the script, which began regular enough, had become increasingly painful. I felt this expressed Naomi's plight: a painful chaos was wreaking havoc with the orderly pattern of her life, leaving it almost unrecognizable. Dr. Levi was caring and observant, yet unconcerned about my perceptions of pain and chaos.

Walking up to Arden's small apartment office on a quiet street adjacent to the Santa Fe art district, I was eager to discuss this dream. I sat alone in the tiny waiting room until he appeared, bidding me to come inside. When we were seated, I talked as usual about what weighed most heavily on my heart—Naomi's terrible circumstances. It seemed a cruel torture was being meted out upon her, and I was forced to watch powerlessly. Arden said, "It is as if you are like Mary, the mother of Jesus, at His feet while He is on the cross."

Then I described my dream, drawing a scratched symbol that I remembered from the last line of Naomi's writing. Arden looked at my sketch inquisitively, then with the air of someone who had just solved a mysterious riddle, he smiled and said, "It's the Greek symbol for logos, found in the Bible, in the first chapter of John, where it says, 'In the beginning was the Word, and the Word was with God, and the Word was God.'" I sat in stunned silence for a moment as my perception shifted, and then replied, "Thank you so much for telling me that. It has changed my impression of the dream completely."

At home, I immediately looked up the first chapter of John in the New Testament, which goes on to read:

The same was in the beginning with God. All things were made by him; and without him was not anything made that was made. In him was life; and the life that was the light of men. And the light shineth in the darkness; and the darkness comprehended it not. [1]

I felt that a hidden truth had miraculously been revealed to me: within Naomi's life were worlds upon worlds. Her suffering was in the name of life, the same as that which is "the light of men." Although there was outward darkness, inwardly the light of life shone.

Then I looked through the Bahá'í writings and found Bahá'u'lláh's description of the nearness of God:

O My servants! The one true God is My witness! This most great, this fathomless and surging Ocean is near, astonishingly near, unto you. Behold it is closer to you than your life-vein! Swift as the twinkling of an eye ye can, if ye but wish it, reach and partake of this imperishable favor, this God-given grace, this incorruptible gift, this most potent and unspeakably glorious bounty. [2]

I puzzled over the difference between the immortal, glorious life close to our souls, and the dark, temporal existence to which our bodies are attached. I pondered what John was implying when he said: "And the light shineth in the darkness; and the darkness comprehended it not." Darkness must be the material world, I thought, which does not comprehend the light. That is why the two youngsters threw the lad off the bridge. Although the light of God shone on them, they did not know it, as if cut off, because the material realm does not comprehend the light—*only the opened inner eye* sees it. Taking this line of thinking further, I discovered that everywhere, the comfort and happiness promised by the material world is merely fleeting, because materiality is by its nature subject to death. Learning the code, however, gives our inner eyes a chance to open, and thus witness the place of deathless splendor. Naomi, I determined, must have already gleaned this awareness for she wrote in her journal, "Everything is illusion back to God," and below it, "Divine order is always in place; we just have to bring our minds to it."

Days later I was working in my studio when Naomi phoned with some shocking news. As usual, she first asked after my own well-being, saying, "Hi, Dad. How are you doing?"

"Fine," I answered. "How are you?"

"I am in the hospital. They found a tumor on my spine, and I am going to get radiation."

My heart sank, and I countered, "But I thought you were not supposed to get any more radiation. Do the doctors know how much you have already had?"

She answered plaintively, knowing my feeling about radiation, "Yes, I am sure they know." Then she explained that Angie and Brent were helping her.

After we hung up, I called my mother, who also was surprised to hear that Naomi was in the hospital. I told her what I knew, then I asked if she would visit Naomi. She agreed to go right away.

Next, I called Naomi back, told her that Grandma was coming over, and asked why she hadn't told her. She replied, "Grandma gets worried easily, and I did not want to upset her."

Finally, I spoke with Angie to see if I was needed. She sounded concerned, and said apologetically, "I think Naomi would like it if you came for a while."

Mentally preparing to drop everything and leave, I called Naomi back. When I asked if I should come out, she replied, "I'll think about it."

I was surprised at her response and fierce strength, but wanting her to remain open to my love and support, I said, "Hey, we have been in this together a long time. You know we're in it together, right?"

"Yes," she answered, then after a pause, added, "I guess I want you to come."

Two days later my father picked me up at the Santa Barbara

airport and drove me to his house as we discussed the help Naomi would need in the coming days. While carrying my suitcase back to the cottage, I passed a blooming jasmine vine, and its dazzling fragrance caused me to stop and inhale deeply, thankful for this momentary pleasure. Then my mother gave me a warm hug, knowing that my heart was breaking.

Soon afterward, my father drove me to Brent's house. Noticing Naomi's gold Toyota compact parked out front, my heaviness evaporated and I was suddenly filled with longing to see my daughter. The front door was open, and there, sitting and reading on the living room couch was Naomi, thinner than ever before. Looking up with wide-open eyes but no smile, she said, "Hi, Dad," and then greeted her grandfather, who invited us both to his house for supper. Throughout this time, Naomi did not move her body. I refrained from saying anything since I knew how much she disliked being asked about her own well-being.

In a short while, Brent arrived and my father left. Then the kids came in, full of energy, and Naomi lit up affectionately as they zoomed around the house playing. When it was time to leave for supper, she stood up and said, "Dad, can you help me?" Holding tightly to my arm, she limped slowly and stiffly down the steps to her car. Softly she explained, "I can't feel my foot anymore." I opened the passenger door, helped her in, and then drove to my parents' house.

Naomi had changed pain medications and was now wearing a patch on her arm that gave her a continual three-day dosage of Duragesic Fentanyl, a strong narcotic with fewer side effects than the morphine-based Roxinal, which had made her slightly nauseated and interfered with her appetite. Radiation treatments were weakening her, and her weight loss had become a serious problem. Eating was a chore rather than a pleasure, and blood tests indicated that she was burning calories quickly and not replenishing them sufficiently. Consequently, Dr. Maas told her, "You have to get those calories!" and prescribed a diet that included meat, supplements, an oral form of shark cartilage, and thymus to aid in her metabolism.

Being cooped up was an almost unbearable limitation for Naomi, an one that she refused to accept. Although she could barely walk and needed a wheelchair to travel from the hospital entrance to the radiation treatment room, she nonetheless wanted to be out and about. Fortunately, the radiation treatments took only a few minutes, and other than on checkup days, we were out of the hospital within half an hour. As a diversion, I continued to paint for my gallery in Santa Fe, finding good spots to go with Naomi, who knew the way to lovely places. Sadly, she was sickened by her treatments and in pain, so she usually would lay on a blanket and read rather than paint beside me. Still, she was happy outdoors, whether at a park, driving around with the windows down, or hanging out at a local café. Despite our daily trips to the hospital and gloomy prospects, Naomi was fighting to keep her ground, and her healers were continuing their help and support. Dr. Allina worked with her on positive imaging, Dr. Maas on her biochemistry, Ann on her muscular-skeletal system, Dr. Gravitz on her emotional and mental self, Chiyen on her energy, and Dr. Hodder on monitoring the cancer and prescribing pain medicine.

One day as we were out driving to appointments and doing errands, we stopped along lower State Street to visit the farmer's market. Several blocks were closed to traffic, and local farmers sat at booths in the middle of the broad avenue, selling flowers, fruits, and vegetables. Naomi was particularly weak and nauseated, yet as usual, determined to get the most out of each moment. Arm-in-arm, we made our way among the booths, but suddenly she felt nauseated and had to sit down on the curb. After a few moments, we started back, and near the walkway to the parking lot, she stopped and said, "You go ahead and buy some flowers for Grandma. I'll wait here." I bought two beautiful California floral bouquets, and when I arrived at Naomi's side again, I noticed a disheveled young man seated on the curb nearby and begging. As we were about to leave, Naomi gazed directly at him and declared loudly and clearly, "You are lucky!" Astonished, the fellow looked up and stared at her! "You have your health," she said before turning away.

I knew I had to be with Naomi until she improved enough to drive again. No one else was prepared to entirely give up their activities and be with her full-time—driving to appointments, helping with shopping and cooking, staying emotionally intimate with someone young and struggling with death. Naomi, however, made it easy for me, by taking me to beautiful places, noticing birds singing, pointing out flowers blooming along the roadside, and reminding me how important people are, and how lucky we were to be alive. Consequently, even with all the chores and the sorrow I felt about her illness, I relished our time together.

After picking up Naomi at Brent's one morning, I drove to a park by the Pacific Ocean. There we got out of the car, and she held on to my left arm as we walked slowly to a sunny spot near the shade of an old tree. Spreading a blanket on the ground, I asked her if she had any recent dreams she felt like sharing.

"Yes," she said, sitting down and telling a dream:

> *I was on top of a building, looking out over a courtyard. There was a figure below in a black hooded cloak. I wanted to get a closer look, so I stepped off the building and swooped down to the ground. It was as if my limbs were elastic. Then the figure turned into a black kitten. I picked it up and squeezed it; I felt bad doing this, but in my mind, the cat was cancer. Then I took it back to the ledge on top of the building. There the kitten became a baby in a white cloth. I unwrapped the bundle and found a boy. There were maggots crawling around his genitals and eyes.*

Remorse and sorrow engulfed me, as I had not thought that my innocent question would elicit such a dark response. With a lump in my throat, I asked Naomi if she knew what the dream might mean. She answered: "I have had dreams before where my limbs were like rubber and I could stretch. The cloaked figure was a sign that I needed to see, and it showed me cancer. That's why I tried to kill the kitten, but I couldn't. When I woke from the dream, I got up, then went back to bed thinking I needed to finish it. I returned to the image of the baby and sent him pure white light filled with total and complete love. Then I watched as the baby turned into sparkling lights that went up into the sky."

I felt grief for the terror of her dream, and I realized that Naomi was no longer a child but rather a wizened adult, seasoned on the battlefield of life. Then I thought, *the strength of the warrior has been passed on to her*, for the gloom of creation was being hurled at her not only in her waking life, but also in her sleep, and as a true warrior, she had become adept at conquering darkness with the sceptre of light. I understood too that she was a young woman who knew war and grief and fought as hard as any grown man on the front line of a vicious battle. I felt that if I must ever be in war, I wanted someone with Naomi's tenacious courage fighting beside me.

My mother had relinquished hope for Naomi's survival, and in her usual blunt way told me that the cancer had "gotten her." Early one evening, she looked up at me from her living room chair and pleaded, "Please, take your baby home." Aware that my mother had asked Naomi numerous times to return to Santa Fe and that Naomi had refused, I replied that it was Naomi who commanded her own destiny—and my job was to honor her choices. Another time, my mother scolded me for praying so much, telling me to "give God a break." But I felt that no one could say how much time Naomi had left in this world, and I continued my supplications for her health, thinking only God knew how much time she had left and He must know of my love for her.

HOPE FOR A MIRACLE

It seems there is no way of knowing that everything is going to be okay. The only thing I can do is trust in God and the power I have within.

R ealizing I needed to stay with Naomi in Santa Barbara, I went to Santa Fe for a short while to prepare for my move to California. As usual, Jean and Sarah had been without me for days on end, and I wondered if Sarah had felt forsaken. Fortunately, Jean had dear supportive friends for company, and Sarah saw a child psychologist once a week. More importantly, our love for Naomi was a common bond among us, so that when I was with her, the reason was understood and upheld by all.

After my short visit home I returned to Santa Barbara, where my father arranged a meeting at his office to discuss the situation that was brewing at Brent's house. Once we had all sat down, Brent looked at me with sad eyes and said that he did not feel Naomi could continue living with them. I tried to stay composed as he elaborated and said, "We have a small house, and Angie hasn't been sleeping well. The other night, Naomi fell while going to the bathroom. We both have pressure in our jobs, and although I want to help, we can't do it much longer. Angie never gets sick, and she has become ill." I realized that Naomi's struggle was a powerful vortex that easily disturbed the balance of life around her and often upset other people.

My father, stressing the need for practicality, suggested I make arrangements for hospice care. But I knew that Dr. Allina had mentioned hospice care to Naomi and she had shunned the thought. Suddenly I broke down crying, admitting I could not concede that Naomi was dying. Even though my father brought up Dr. Hodder's belief that she might only have two months to live, I stood with her in her hope; if she had faith, then I too stayed faithful. As an alternative, Brent finally agreed to let Naomi stay with them while I looked for an apartment to share with her.

My hope continued to be buttressed by many stories of cancer survivors whose prognoses the medical establishment had considered hopeless. For example, Naomi met Ginny Walden, a middle-aged Santa Fe artist who was successfully battling advanced breast cancer. After completing chemo and radiation, Ginny had become a Qigong teacher, and she sent Naomi books and tapes to assist her in Chi-Lel practice. Chi-Lel derives from Qigong, condensing the 5,000-year-old practice of cultivating life-force energy into a few select methods of subtle movements that enhance the mind-body connection. One book, *101 Miracles of Natural Healing* by Luke Chan, was a collection of true testimonials from a renowned healing center in Qinhuangdao, China, of 101 people who overcame a wide variety of serious illnesses by practicing Chi-Lel. Another, simply titled *100 Days* and written by Janet Graham, a friend of Ginny's, recounted the author's experience after being told she had only a few days to live. Following a phone conversation with her one afternoon, Naomi told me that Janet had initially battled breast cancer, which spread to 80 percent of her liver. As a last resort, the doctors inserted a tube into her liver to reduce the edema, and Janet survived. Now she practiced Qigong daily and promulgated its health benefits.

About this time, we also gained hope when we heard of an unusual healer in San Francisco. Jean learned from a friend about a woman named Jane who had been diagnosed with breast cancer that spread to over 70 percent of her bones, whereupon her doctors told her she had only three months to live. She refused traditional medical treatment, and very sick, she sought treatment from the Dalai Lama's personal physician in San Francisco. But the herbs she was given made her feel sicker. Then a friend told her that she had been cured of cancer by a healer from Russia named Andrei Aleshov, who was living nearby. Following an interview and trial treatment period, Jane, who was by now extremely emaciated and in a wheelchair, began seeing Andrei for daily therapy. Miraculously, after months of treatment, the progress of her cancer had been reversed and she could walk again.

I tracked down Jane's phone number and called her, incredulous that such a story could possibly be true. "I put my whole life in his hands," she said. When I asked about Andrei's approach, she could only tell me he worked "astrally." After thanking her for speaking with me, and promising to pray for her, I hung up, feeling like her experience was almost unreal, even dreamlike.

Later, Naomi spoke with Jane and learned that Andrei received calls between 10:00 and 11:00 A.M. on weekdays, so she called him, explaining that she had cancer and wanted to see him. In a thick Russian accent he asked where the cancer was and if she would like him to work on her now. As she held the phone to her ear, Naomi felt a powerful energy around her and a tingling in her left hip. Finally, Andrei told her to call him back after she had finished radiation, because he did not see clients receiving other forms of therapy.

My father was skeptical of Andrei's ability to cure Naomi and, using his extensive connections around the country, began making inquiries. After some sleuthing, a psychiatrist friend reported that years earlier Andrei had participated in a study of people claiming alternative healing powers, but had been unable to "see" a metal plate in the leg of a man presented to him as a test subject. Hearing this, my father was even more dubious. One Sunday afternoon in March, we rested on lawn chairs by my parents' garden and talked, while the sun blazed overhead. My father sat in his shorts, shirtless, with his bare feet in the grass. When the conversation turned to Andrei, he let loose a puff of smoke from his cigar, narrowed his eyes, and said, "I do not want Naomi to get her hopes up and then be tricked by a charlatan."

I understood his point, and answered that we didn't have many options left. "Besides," I added, "it seems to me a charlatan makes claims so he can get your money and run. So far, Andrei has not even mentioned money and does not seem concerned about getting it."

Meanwhile, my mother continued pleading for Naomi's return to Santa Fe, saying, "Jean and Sarah are there. All her friends are there." But I knew Naomi would not be persuaded to go home, and I was not about to try and force her, opting as always to support her determination and hope.

By now the radiation had helped Naomi regain more of her mobility, so I no longer put her in a wheelchair when we went into the hospital; instead, she walked holding on to my arm. But unfortunately, her nausea had increased, and she threw up after eating. Her weight dropped to ninety-five pounds. Determined not to be emaciated, she forced herself to eat, albeit slowly.

Although it was difficult, she could now climb the Brodes' front steps again, so she moved back in with them while I went house hunting. In addition to gaining mobility, she was also developing more perspective on her tragic situation. One day during a visit to the beach with my father, Naomi watched as people jogged up and down the shoreline. Seeing a group of laughing youngsters full of exuberant life pass by, she confided to him, "I used to get angry feeling that I can't do fun things like others, but I've gotten over it."

Jean's fiftieth birthday was April 1, and despite my desire to celebrate this milestone with her, I simply could not. Calling to apologize for not being with her, I explained that while she could look forward to many more birthday celebrations, Naomi might not. Her range of movement was returning, but she was sickened and struggled to keep up with her therapies. I *had* to be with her.

Shortly afterward, Jean and Sarah flew out to join us for a week. We all stayed at Brent's house while his family took a weekend trip to Las Vegas. Immediately upon her arrival, Jean was ready to be of service to Naomi in whatever way she could, but Naomi insisted on her comfortable familiarity with me. We suspected she wanted with all her heart to be seen as a normal teenager instead of someone with cancer. She even admitted to acting as if she were okay when she really felt terrible, explaining that whenever she said she felt bad, people hovered over her, suffocatingly. This dynamic was difficult for us because we looked to her for guidance in determining how best to be helpful. Nevertheless, Naomi remained steadfast in maintaining that she was doing fine and avoided any conversation about her condition.

Near the end of Jean and Sarah's stay, while Jean and Naomi were in the car one day after a radiation treatment, Naomi asked, "So, have you had a good time on your visit here?"

Jean answered, "Yes, I have, but it was a little hard for me in the beginning."

Naomi said, "Well, I think what happened was that you were trying a little too hard and I wasn't trying hard enough!"

Jean later commented that this kind of balanced observation and shared responsibility for conflict was a new step for Naomi and it revealed an aspect of her transformation. Excited to have witnessed this unexpected leap forward, Jean saw it as a fruit born of Naomi's amazing courage and glowing sense of hope.

SONG FROM THE MOUNTAINTOPS

May I be protected from internal and external harm,
May I be healthy and strong,
May I be happy and at peace,
May I care for myself joyfully.

One evening around suppertime, I was at my parents' house when Jean called from Santa Fe and said, "Andrei is going to be on a program called *Unsolved Mysteries* that starts in a few minutes. Be sure to watch it." Scrambling for the newspaper, I scoured the day's television listings, but found no mention of *Unsolved Mysteries*.

The next morning, I called Jean back to get her impressions of Andrei. She said, "I was surprised, because he looked really different from what I expected. He's quite heavy and very young looking. A couple went to him with their two-year-old daughter who had a brain tumor. She had undergone numerous surgeries but each time, the cancer came back. Andrei began working with her, and although his work made her nauseated, he reassured the family that changes were to be expected and were part of the healing process. He continued working with her for some months, and now she is five years old and healthy." Happy to hear more validation about Andrei, I told my mother about his work. Surprisingly, she said, "Anything can happen in this world. We don't know." I was glad to hear this acknowledgement from her, since she had been pessimistic in her pragmatic way. Gratefully, I accepted that she was allowing room for hope.

Difficulties regarding Naomi's care grew and my emotional life became more profound because of our struggle. With regard to housing, we were in a bind. To rent an apartment in Santa Barbara was expensive, and we hoped to go to San Francisco and work with Andrei as soon as possible. My father felt I needed hospice assistance with Naomi, but she was living so fully in hope and faith that I could not bear to call on them. Despite all the complications of our lives, Naomi stirred up the depths of my feelings each day, and whether I was with her or not, my thoughts turned to her constantly. We struggled together, sharing victories and defeats. She looked forward to her appointments with the healers each day and eagerly made new friends. I marveled at her resilience and her capacity to begin each day with anticipation despite her pain and the formidable odds against her. She charged forward with hope, love, and determination as true warriors do, and I barely managed to keep up with her, finally welcoming sleep at night.

Now when I retired after saying prayers, my dreams increasingly reflected the day's tension. Often it seemed I was in a maze with no way out. Then I had an unusually uplifting yet disturbing dream:

I was in a bucolic field in the early evening. The air was soft and silken; everything felt serene and etheric. As I stood enveloped in the twilight, I heard a chorus of voices. Then gazing over the shrouded hills, I saw mountains wrapped in a gentle, golden light, and I traced the singing to their peaks. In front of me, and also looking up at the mountains, was a man dressed in the garb of nobility—a silver robe and turban, both with black stripes. He stood at rapt attention, and then leaning slightly to the right, he slowly bent his head to hear better the glorious chorus coming from the mountaintops, beckoning me by his example to be reverently attentive. A moment later a blissfulness came over me as I heard the holy ones sing, "We say it. We say it."

Upon waking, I sensed that I had been given a gift, and yet felt fearful of this holy edict decreed in the words, "We say it. We say it." Was the holy spirit giving me a glimpse of the next world, and was this a preview of Naomi's ultimate dwelling place? If so, I concluded, nothing would keep her in this world. Then I remembered two paintings she had recently completed, both entirely in shades of blue. One depicted a man releasing a bird from his hands and watching it fly upward. Around his head were swirling lights reminiscent of van Gogh's *Starry Night*. The other painting was of a group of singers, amorphous figures standing together in a choir, featureless except for open mouths. Wondering if she was already communing with the heavenly host, I realized that Naomi did not belong to me or this world, but to them. Inexplicably, I felt great sadness come over me, and I sensed simultaneously that her struggle was over and not over.

It seemed Naomi was hanging on by a thread, an amazingly strong one woven of her love and determination. Battered and sick from radiation, fighting the pain of cancer, and rarely sleeping well, she greeted each day as a miracle to relish. The radiation treatments were taking effect, and with a slight return to her former mobility, she managed to keep all her appointments and even suggested places to visit and things to do.

One day we set out on a painting trip together, stopping first at a market for picnic provisions. Then Naomi directed me north over a mountain pass, along a road she had come upon previously while driving on her own. After about twenty minutes of meandering through the grassy countryside dotted

*"Untitled" oil painting
by Naomi
1998*

with trees and flowering shrubs, we came to a secluded state park alongside shimmering Lake Cachuma. With Naomi holding on to my arm, we walked across a footbridge to a tiny deserted island jutting into the lake. While she set down her bag with watercolors and tape player, I spread a blanket over the tall grasses. Flowers were everywhere, and sunlight played across the rippling water. A soft, steady breeze swept through the trees, sounding like the ocean rushing onto a sandy shoreline. After Naomi had settled comfortably on the blanket, beneath the spreading limbs of an old oak tree, I went back across the footbridge and began composing a picture of the little bridge with the island and lake behind it. Using a pencil, I sketched in the outline of the major forms I saw, and after mixing colors on my palette, I applied them directly to my canvas with the palette knife, giving the work texture along with the nuances of colors.

When I had finished my small oil painting, I packed and went to Naomi, who was stretched out on the blanket with her earphones on, practicing Chi-Lel. A small, unfinished watercolor lay by her side. Taking off her earphones and looking up, she asked, "How did your painting go?"

"It's good—I'll show it to you back at the car. How have you been?" I answered.

"I threw up again," she said, exasperated. "It really makes me mad. I tried to eat slowly, but it didn't work."

I helped her up, and as she held on to my arm for support, we walked over to an old tree beside the lake and gazed at the light playing like dazzling diamonds on its windswept surface. "It is so beautiful," she said, after a long moment of silence. "We must come here again to paint."

The beautiful scene captivated me. But even more enthralling was Naomi's longing for wholeness, which had her continually connecting the dots of life and searching for the blessed "big picture" of God's creation, as if when all the dots were finally strung together, she would surely be healed. Gathering our things as the sun threw its late afternoon light all around us, causing the trees and tall grasses to blaze golden amidst the violet shadows, we left grateful and contented.

As we walked into the hospital on Naomi's last day of radiation, she still clutched my arm for support, but her movement seemed much better. After the treatment, we met with the nurse and the doctor. Naomi was weighed, and we saw that she was still about ninety-five pounds. To bolster her caloric intake, the staff gave her canned nutritional drinks called Ensure, which contained up to 360 calories per serving. She liked the taste, and although they were not organic, she drank them to maintain her weight. At last, with a prescription for pain medication in hand, we left the hospital for the last time. Stepping out from the drab, air-conditioned hallways into the bright sun and warm air, Naomi breathed a sigh of relief and said, "Let's go to a park."

We were now pinning our hopes on Andrei. Even Dr. Allina admitted that medically there was nothing left to do and our only recourse was a "shamanic" type of healing. Regrettably, Naomi had called Andrei several times and he seemed to be putting her off. Discouraged, a woman in the healing community went to bat for her, leaving an urgent message on his answering machine: "Do you know how seriously ill Naomi is? If you are a responsible healer, you must see her!" The next time Naomi called, Andrei answered the phone, and since she had finished radiation, he agreed to see her but insisted she call him on Tuesday. I was annoyed, since Naomi's plight seemed like an emergency.

Frustrated by her inability to get an appointment with Andrei and by the urgency of her condition, Naomi wanted to go to San Francisco right away and try to see him without an appointment. I agreed to go with her, so we drove north from Santa Barbara in the late afternoon a few days later. Naomi and I were bonded tightly together in spirit and even felt an ebullient happiness as we faced the unknown.

After spending the night in a Salinas motel, we finally reached San Francisco just before 11:00 A.M. Remembering that Andrei took calls only between 10:00 and 11:00 A.M., Naomi immediately called him from a pay phone. To our surprise and chagrin, he asked her why she hadn't shown up for her appointment on Tuesday, and then told her that he could not see her for at least a week. Neither of us could fathom what had happened, other than a misunderstanding due to his thick Russian accent. Calling him back immediately, I pleaded to be seen as soon as possible but had to settle for a late-afternoon phone conversation. Next I called Jean in Santa Fe, and she was incredulous that we had missed our appointment—a golden opportunity. How could Naomi have misunderstood that she had been given an appointment? "Oh well," I said, "at least we are here, and we are talking with him."

Standing on the corner and trying to get our bearings, we looked around us. I studied a map of San Francisco and plotted a path to the Seal Rock Inn at the end of Geary Street, where we had booked a room for several nights. The Seal Rock Inn is an older, three-story hotel with views of the Pacific Ocean. We had found it while browsing through a travel guide in Santa Barbara; it wasn't very expensive and was located near Andrei's home office. Between the hotel and the ocean was Sutro Park, a small city common with broad gravel walks, flower beds, lawns, cyprus trees, and a spectacular coastal overlook. The air was chilly, with steady breezes. After checking in, I helped Naomi into the musty elevator and pushed the button for the second floor. We arrived at a balcony that followed the L-shape of the building, above an inner courtyard with a Ping-Pong table and tiny swimming pool. Our room, which had old beige carpeting, and prints of San Francisco scenery, offered a view of the bus stop, and beyond it we could see the park and the ocean. I put the thymus and shark cartilage in the freezer portion of the little refrigerator, and called Andrei, leaving a message where we could be reached.

Later that afternoon while Naomi rested, I went out alone to survey the neighborhood. Most buildings were only two or three stories high and seemed to grow out of the sidewalk, making front yards, much less lawns, an impossibility, and trees a rarity. Geary Street and the parallel thoroughfares were wall-to-wall shops; many advertised their wares in Asian or Russian writing over the front doors. The streets perpendicular to these business avenues were crammed with homes and apartments. Every block, streets and avenues alike, seemed to be sloping on a hill, so that I was trekking either up or down. Circling around this rollercoaster to the higher vantage point of Geary Street, I could see the great trees of Golden Gate Park. When I returned to the room, Naomi reported that Andrei had called and given her a brief session over the phone. She could feel him working, but not as strongly as before. Grateful that he had called and spent time with Naomi, I began to trust him.

Weekends at the Seal Rock Inn were booked solid well in advance, which meant that we had to arrange other accommodations during those times. Driving around the area, Naomi and I found the Great Highway Motor Inn, which we moved to on weekends. Over the next month, we shuttled back and forth between the Seal Rock Inn and the Motor Inn.

Naomi continued her phone sessions with Andrei, looking forward to the day when she could see him. Her leg, still painful, was now quite swollen, further hindering her ability to walk. For relief, she began propping it up whenever possible either with pillows or, while in the car, by stretching out on the backseat and putting her left foot out the window. We bought some special support stockings worn by pregnant women with circulation problems, and these seemed to work well. Bothered by the tightness around her unswollen leg, Naomi, accustomed to remedial action, cut off the right stocking.

Once, when her pain medication wore off before the Santa Barbara doctors had renewed her prescription, I saw the raw suffering that afflicted her. As the day went on, she grimly fought the constant agonizing torture and I watched her usual positive personality change to that of a wounded animal. Finally, in our motel room late in the afternoon, she reached into her bag of vitamins and herbal remedies, found a vial of morphine-based Roxinal, swallowed half a dropperful, then curled into a ball on her bed. I stood in the half darkened room as my brave child, dressed in blue jeans and brown cotton sweater, lay motionless on her side. Sadly, I realized how unbearable living had become for her. How could a loving God allow *this?* Yet in the deepest part of my soul, I knew that we had not been abandoned but rather had been given a supreme test. Reaching for my copy of *Gleanings from the Writings of Bahá'u'lláh,* I read:

> *Know ye that trials and tribulations have, from time immemorial been the lot of the chosen Ones of God and His beloved, and such of His servants as are detached from all else but Him, they whom neither merchandise nor traffic beguile from the remembrance of the Almighty, they that speak not till He hath spoken, and act according to His commandment. Such is God's method carried into effect of old, and such will it remain in the future. Blessed are the steadfastly enduring, they that are patient under ills and hardships, who lament not over anything that befalleth them, and who tread the path of resignation.* [1]

At last the phone rang, and the owner of the motel told me that a priority letter had arrived for us. I ran to the office, where I was relieved to find the prescription we had been waiting for, and then I went to a drugstore and bought the Fentanyl Duragesic patches. Back at the motel room, Naomi got up, pulled off her sweater, and opened the box. Because her body had become accustomed to the medicine, the 100 mg dose she had begun in Santa Barbara was increased to 200 mg. Peeling the foil wrapping off two patches, she slapped them on her arm over the sticky residue from the former patches. In a short while the patches began providing relief, and we went in search of a Chinese carry-out restaurant.

After placing our order, I could hear in the back of my mind, words uttered by my college philosophy professor: "The more you want, the more you lack." How appropriate, I thought, recognizing that my desire for Naomi's healing was so dense and weighted that I easily sank beneath the ocean of life. The more we wanted her wellness, and the more remedial steps we took, the greater was our awareness that we could not effect a cure. It seemed our most awesome task was now at hand. We must learn the code and surrender to the ocean of God's eternity, abandoning ourselves to His will, however scary it might seem. Sitting in the restaurant with my beloved daughter, I vowed to do my best to remember the song from the mountaintops each time I noticed life slipping away from her. As for Naomi, she loved the world and hoped God would give her longer to live in it.

Andrei

Oh Lord! I ask to be full of you and empty of cancer.
Thank you for giving me the greatest gift of yourself, and God,
please accept my gratitude for fuller reception of you
and greater freedom from the usurper's plague.
Hosana, Amen, and Thanks

Naomi continued the practice of Chi-Lel that she had begun in Santa Barbara under the guidance of Chiyen. From the center of her being, whether in the motel room or the car, she meditated on bringing clear, healing chi energy into her body. Further, at night before going to sleep, she did visualization exercises, using anatomical drawings of skeletons and lungs to send energy through her body. With a yellow, or red magic marker, she colored in the bones and lungs, symbolically infusing them with light and life, then filled the rest of the page with affirmations. As she sat up in bed with pillows behind her back, page after moving page flew from her pen. One night she wrote:

My bones and tissues are full of chi—my body is chi! All cancer cells are gone! I believe that I have the ability to overcome cancer with the help of God and chi—God and chi are one! The life force is chi. I thank God in advance for this miracle of healing that He has given me, the miracle of being cancer free, able to do the things that I want to again. I believe in myself! I am strong! I am healthy! I have the ability to speak my truth, what I believe in, to whomever. I love and appreciate myself completely.

She was using warrior strength to overcome fear and doubt, and in my mind I knew she was flooding all the dark places with light.

Another night she penned:

There is no fear in my body! Chi is filling my entire body! Love, joy, and happy thoughts fill my mind. I am happy! All cells in my body feel joy and life energy, and have the ability to get rid of the cancer. I am thankful to God for the miracles of health and healing He is giving me. I ask the cancer to leave now. All cancer cells are gone! Bones are strong. I am strong! Chi and blood are plentiful inside. I ask that chi moves easily through the left side of my body. My body is happy and my body is healthy now. Bone marrow, immune system, bones, body are all strong, healthy, and able to get rid of cancer! I am happy that it is so!

Naomi, the strong warrior, was sitting on her powerful horse, a red stallion symbolizing life, and summoning it to battle.

Still another time she wrote:

I am chi. I am full of the life force, full of the flowers, trees, the smells of lavender and roses, the feelings of the wind blowing against my face as I run, and the wonder when I go snorkeling and see the other world! That is only a little bit of what the life force is. I am chi, that life force. I am healed; I am thankful to God for healing me! I am thankful to God for getting rid of the cancer! Blood and chi are plentiful! Thank you, Lord!

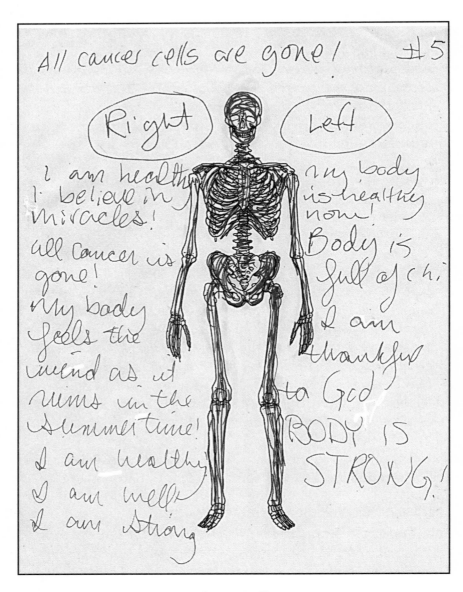

A page of Naomi's affirmations

She was calling on the force within all of life, the same force she had expressed as a child when she drew pictures of smiling children standing on the brown earth, their sturdy homes nearby, and flowers blooming under the loving rays of a warm sun, their roots firmly anchored in the soil below.

Often, Naomi would end her writing by drawing a picture on the back of one of the pages. Once, she drew a picture of herself eating and beside it wrote, "Me, eating a bunch (of food), three times, and snacks!" Another night, she drew an artist at an easel and wrote, "Me at art school! Healthy, cancer free!" On yet another night she drew two couples holding hands and wearing backpacks, and then wrote, "I am healthy, joyful, and happy with my friends in Europe. We are backpacking, the way I have always dreamed!"

As a way of diverting ourselves from anxiety, we went on daily excursions, visiting such places as the campus of California College of Arts and Crafts, where Naomi was to begin classes in September. While we strolled around the small, well-landscaped grounds, exploring classrooms, speaking with summer students, and anticipating the beginning of fall classes, Naomi gripped my arm and remarked, "Isn't it a beautiful campus?" Later she confided that she had felt uneasy lest her counselor might see her holding on to my arm for support.

Finding a parking place on the crowded streets was challenging. If I became frustrated by the scarcity of parking, Naomi would remind me to "visualize an empty space." The funny thing was—it usually worked.

Nearby Golden Gate Park became another favorite place to spend time, seeming always to welcome us, like a gracious, loyal friend greets weary travelers. After one visit Naomi wrote the following E-mail to her friend Adella in Santa Fe:

Dear Adella,

Hey there, how are you? I am in San Francisco with my dad. We came up here to see that Russian Dr. I don't know if I told you about him or not. San Fran. is totally cool. Have you ever been here? You would absolutely love it! There is so much to see and so much to do all the time. My dad and I went to Golden Gate Park, which is the most amazing park you will ever see. You drive in, and there is a windmill from the 1800s with beautiful tulips, poppies, and gorgeous trees surrounding it. We looked at the map that they have for the public and decided to go see another portion of the park that had some kind of flower that my dad had heard of and that I had never heard of. On our way, we saw buffalo, waterfalls, beautiful old trees, an aquarium, and a botanical garden (we did not actually go in to see those, but we saw signs for them). As we drove along, there were little and big meadows with blossoming trees and bushes ranging from white to bright, bright red. Then we decided to go see the Japanese Tea Garden, which was absolutely beautiful. There were miniature trees, little paths that were lined with bamboo railings (the railings come up to your knees, so they are really quite useless but give a nice touch), blooming bushes—reds, yellows, purples, pinks, whites, and every shade of green you can imagine. There were many little ponds and a big one that had goldfish. There were cool statues all over the place, and my favorite one was of a huge Buddha. So that was really cool.

We have not been to the art museums but plan to go. Also, we want to go over the Golden Gate Bridge and see the redwoods. We went to see my art school—cool.

Some of the roads are sooooo steep it is unbelievable . . . one of those things that you just have to see.

Well, I will talk to you soon. I love you!

Naomi

Wherever we went, we carried Luke Chan's *101 Miracles of Natural Healing*, which contained such remarkable stories of recuperation from seemingly hopeless conditions that I had a hard time believing them. On the other hand, I thought, maybe miracles happen so that nonbelievers become believers.

Our San Francisco experience—thus far a heady mix of excitement, struggle, anticipation, pain, and joy—took another twist one night. We had retired around 10:30 P.M., and unbeknownst to us, Naomi's painkiller patches were nearly expired. So all night she tossed and turned in excruciating pain. Aware of her torture and unable to help, I lay awake in anguish, and when I heard her fumbling for aspirin and saw her swallow three, in frustration I said, "Naomi, I can't do this by myself anymore. We need to go home. We *have* to go home!" After a few moments of thoughtful silence, she answered, "Maybe you're right." In the morning, after only a few hours of sleep, she put new patches on and we set off for a grungy but comfortable coffee shop near the beach. As we drove away from the Seal Rock Inn, Naomi looked at me and said, "You almost got me last night!" In my head I heard her saying, "I am not going home, and you might as well know it!" Admiring her spunk, I felt a quirky smile creep across my face.

Finally, after waiting two weeks, Andrei gave us an appointment, which bolstered our spirits. On the day of our appointment, we were both a little nervous as we approached his home, a typical San Francisco house—white, three stories high, with a gabled roof, and stairs leading from the sidewalk to a landing at the front door. To the right of the door, a picture window with half-closed venetian blinds faced the street. At the corner, we could see the huge, old trees lining the Fulton Street entrance to the Golden Gate Park. Holding on to the railing, Naomi slowly climbed the stairs and then rang the doorbell. Very soon the door swung open, revealing a tall, swarthy, very heavy, dark-haired man. He stood straight, with his belly rolling over his belt, threatening to pop the lower buttons of his brown-and-black paisley shirt. His face and hands were fleshy, and his left eye strayed to the side ever so slightly. Greeting us with barely a smile, he waved us into the living room, saying in a deep, velvety voice that seemed to dislike the effort of putting syllables together in English, "Please, come in." The living room appeared too small for him, let alone others as well. A shag throw-rug lay on the wood floor, and on a mantel above the fireplace were snapshots of good-looking people standing with him, all smiling for the photographer. On the walls hung large paintings of mysterious figures with big eyes, erect in a swirling cosmos. The furniture was mostly made of twisted and polished slabs of dark cedar. And oddly, a parrot in the room behind us stepped around in its cage, cocking its head to and fro as if angling for a better view of us.

Andrei had Naomi sit on a small, straight-backed chair in the center of the room, facing the picture window, and then he directed me to a cedar chair in front of the window, facing Naomi. He then asked Naomi if she had any questions, to which she replied, "No." Next, he stepped behind her, grabbed a remote control, and clicked on what seemed like eerie synthesized music—mostly string-sounding notes that melodically rose and fell, and repeatedly looped back on themselves. While the music played, Andrei leaned over Naomi, reaching around her upper body and grasping the air that surrounded her. Swaying back and forth while using both hands, he seemed to be feeling the space around her. Occasionally a shaking hand would flick downward and away, as if ridding her energy field of something. His eyes, open and trancelike, appeared to be searching for something invisible. During this time, Naomi sat still and erect, eyes shut, obviously sensing the energetic currents now swirling around her.

After about ten minutes, Andrei clicked off the music and asked Naomi, "What did you feel?"

Opening her eyes, Naomi was silent a moment, then answered, "It felt like my leg twitched. I could feel tingling."

Leaning over a desk to write in his appointment book, Andrei said "Good, good," in a singsong way, then handed Naomi a slip of paper indicating the time of her appointment the next day. At the front door, he smiled and said good-bye. Naomi asked if she could give him a hug. Taken aback, he stood still, with his right hand on the now open door. She leaned her thin body forward, wrapped her arms around his huge waist, and gave a squeeze.

Thus began our daily visits with Andrei. We never knew more

than a day in advance what time our appointment would be, since he was seeing people every fifteen minutes between 11:00 A.M. and 4:00 P.M. on weekdays. When I asked about payment, he dismissed the idea, saying he was not sure yet if he would accept Naomi as a regular patient, that he first needed to know if she responded well.

A few days later as we were leaving, I said, "God bless you."

"No, I don't believe," he replied. Then seeing my surprise, he gestured toward Naomi and said in his broken English, "Otherwise, if there is God, why is this happen to her? It should happen to someone bad. Why it happen to her?" I could not answer him, especially as our time was up, so I smiled and said good-bye. Later, I reflected on the fact that some people believe in God and some don't. I have known many who have said outright that they couldn't believe in God because of the bad things that happen in life. Yet throughout our ordeal, I had never lost my faith that somehow Naomi was in a loving embrace, that we were not alone, that our prayers were heard even though they were answered in ways that were hard to comprehend, and that after all, this life was simply a drama unfolding into the next life.

Bahá'u'lláh, expressing words from God, had commented on this lack of belief when He said,

> *O Children of the Divine and Invisible Essence!*
> *Ye shall be hindered from loving Me and souls shall be perturbed*
> *as they make mention of Me. For minds cannot grasp Me nor hearts*
> *contain Me.* [1]

We had heard that Andrei required a two-week trial period before accepting someone as a patient, but waiting for a verdict was hard to bear. It seemed we were casting about desperately in a deep sea, with the thinnest of margins separating life from death. Naomi was concentrating entirely on life, putting all her trust and faith in God and willing herself to heal. I felt strong but strangely fragile and weak at the same time. And anxious as well. The sight of her thin body and swollen leg pained me. Alone, I began smoking ciga-rettes—four or five a day to calm the effects of stress. Naomi could tell if I had lit up in her car, and she would scold me, though she understood my anguish and need for relief. If I left the motel room to go outside for a smoke, she would ask, "What upset you this time?" One morning after I had come back from smoking a ciga-rette, Naomi looked at me and said, "I have been thinking about you, wondering what would help. It occurred to me that we are strongest when we are happy. Just be happy and smile—it is heal-ing!" She was right of course, but how could I feel happy and des-perate at the same time? I was embarrassed at my weakness and could not tell her that I worried over her, that my unrelieved anxi-ety stemmed from powerlessness, that I was distraught because she was dying. Responding to my unspoken thoughts, she said with loving compassion, "Dad, if you are stressed, just pray."

One Sunday we took a drive over the Golden Gate Bridge through Sausalito and on to the Muir Woods. It was a beautiful day with temperatures in the seventies, and people of all ages and nation-alities were out strolling on the bridge. On our approach to Sau-salito, we traveled through a tunnel. Then following the curving road over the hills, we passed a sign that read, "White Cloud Zen Center," tucked in a glade of eucalyptus trees. The air streaming in our windows carried pungent fragrances of grass, flowers, leafy oils, and moist, rich earth.

When we reached the redwood forest of Muir Woods, we walked slowly arm-in-arm along a broad footpath under the immense trees. Typically I walk so briskly that Jean accuses me of charging ahead mercilessly. Now, forced to go very slowly alongside my daughter, I gained a new awareness of life. The redwoods them-selves seemed to carry the same message: there is no hurry to grow older. Absorbing the presence of the towering great ones that had been rooted to their spots through cold and hot weather for over a thousand years, I said to myself, "Thank you, Naomi, for making me slow down." At one point we stood still, drinking in the air and feeling safe among these silent witnesses. Then continuing on with occasional pauses, we looped back almost to where we had started. As we stopped beside a stream, Naomi pointed to a fallen tree that had new shoots coming out of its rotting trunk. The shoots grew upward toward the sky, showing through a break in the canopy far above. "Isn't that amazing, Dad?" she asked. "That one has fallen down, and a new one is growing out of it!"

Naomi never ceased to inspire me with her insightful observations, finding the beautiful in life despite the ugly pain of cancer. Now, as she observed life resurrecting itself in the form of a tender shoot emerging from a decaying log, I was reminded of the story of Jesus, who one day was walking with His disciples when they came upon the rotting corpse of a dog. The disciples, wishing to spare their master the gruesome sight, made haste to turn away from the scene, but Jesus stepped closer, commenting on the beautiful whiteness of the animal's teeth.

By this time the afternoon was growing late, so we headed back to San Francisco. Just before the tunnel, traffic slowed to a crawl since people who had gone north on Sunday outings were returning to the city. As we entered the tunnel, we heard a horn honking and then another and yet another until the cement walls had become a loud echo chamber. A moment later some kids in a convertible honked and began shouting, "Whew! Yippee!" Infected by the rowdiness, I honked my horn, then laughing, Naomi and I shouted, "Yippee!" at the same time.

Later that night at the Seal Rock Inn, after getting ready for bed and saying prayers together, Naomi remarked that it had been a good day. I reflected on the intensity of our current situation. Every waking moment seemed full of drama and yet passed swiftly. There was no doubt that Naomi's life was blazing now, and each day was a dance in the fire, the moments burning up as quickly as they came.

AS YOUR FAITH IS

I ask to be full of you, God,
and empty of cancer.

When we visited Andrei, I sometimes doubted that he could cure Naomi, although it was obvious *something* transpired during treatments since both Naomi and I experienced energy shifts. Several times I even felt dizzy and nauseated afterward. Yet a shadowy feeling plagued me constantly, causing tension and sometimes clouding my thoughts.

I had discussed with Arden Fisk the terrible anxiety associated with my doubt. In the Bahá'í writings it is said, "As your faith is, so shall your powers and blessings be." My faith had always been that Naomi would overcome her foe and live, but the signs of her dying made me feel powerless, throwing me into a swirling vortex of emotions. We had been fighting for life for two years now, but death was still stalking us and seeming to mock our feeble efforts. In my sessions with Arden, he tried to help me accept death, saying that if I continued to resist it, my anxiety would only increase. He explained, "You can accept death without giving up *hope*," but the words made no sense to me, for I could not let go of Naomi, even when all appeared lost. Faith was nothing without conviction to give it wings.

Fortunately, one day I received an overarching insight into suffering in a way that both calmed and challenged me. While immersed in the Bahá'í writings, I came upon a deeply moving passage by Bahá'u'lláh, and as with so many of His divine teachings, my heart and soul grasped the truth, but my mind was slower to catch on. The prayer, in which He recounts His sufferings, ends with these words:

> *Let not thy soul grieve over that which God hath rained down upon Us. Merge thy will in His pleasure, for We have, at no time, desired anything whatsoever except His Will, and have welcomed each one of His irrevocable decrees. Let thine heart be patient, and be thou not dismayed. Follow not in the way of them that are sorely agitated.* [1]

After reading this passage, I felt that my teacher—who, despite His noble heritage, had all His wealth taken from Him, was cast into a foul underground prison for two years with heavy chains around His neck while thousands of His devoted followers were murdered, was poisoned by His enemy, separated from His family, exiled, and then again cast into prison for forty years—was by His example and words encouraging me to be patient rather than agitated. Still, I was in the grips of love and pain, forced to watch helplessly while precious Naomi was being viciously devoured by cancer. Because of my inner turmoil, I felt overly challenged by the counsel to refrain from being sorely agitated. Even so, on some deeper level my soul understood the wisdom of Bahá'u'lláh: we are all immortals standing in the eternal light of a loving God, however dark the *outer* world may be. Naomi was protected, and all was well. Outwardly, my precious flower was withering to death, causing me great alarm and sorrow; inwardly she was blossoming into a fragrant plant of unsurpassed beauty.

About this time my birthday was approaching, and Jean called to tell me that if I wanted to come home, Naomi's friend Maria would stay with her in San Francisco. Maria, a slender young woman with a pale complexion, lively brown eyes, and straight brown hair, had been friends with Naomi ever since their days together at the Waldorf school. Although they had not seen much of each other during Naomi's illness, they had continued their friendship through E-mail.

I told Jean I was not sure how comfortable I would feel coming home right now and I needed a few days to think it over. Naomi seemed fine with the idea and understood that I needed an occasional break. But we had not yet heard of Andrei's plans, and I was concerned about what would happen if, while I was away, he told Naomi he would not see her anymore. So I reviewed Naomi's options with her, emphasizing that the Santa Barbara healing team was still there for her and her Chi-Lel practice was strong. Then I asked what she would do if Andrei declined to see her, and she replied, "Me and Maria would drive back to Santa Barbara together."

Naomi, although apparently living on vapors, seemed stronger than I, perhaps because she had come to terms with the possibility of her death. I, on the other hand, was in constant struggle over it and consequently exhausted. So I trusted that she would be all right with her friend as an assistant for a short while. That evening I told Jean I would come home May 12, the day before my birthday, and would stay two weeks, adding that it might be good for Naomi to have a fresh start with Maria and for me to replenish and renew myself.

At first Naomi seemed shocked that I would be gone for two weeks, but soon I could see her adjusting. She said, "It's that I feel safe with you, Dad." Gathering her courage, a few moments later she added, "Never mind, I'll be all right." Although uncertain about the wisdom of leaving, I decided to trust her strength.

Jean's parents, Mary and Charles, both in their seventies, wanted to visit Naomi over the four days before my departure. Charles, a Harvard Law School graduate, had retired from his own law firm and now worked part-time as a court mediator for the federal government. Mary, a homemaker, did volunteer work at a local hospital. Though not related, Naomi had always called them Grandma and Grandpa, and they treated her as a cherished granddaughter.

Naomi happily agreed to this visit, so I made reservations for them at the Fairmont Hotel. Their four-day visit would end May 12, the day of my departure, and Maria would arrive the day before.

The Sunday before our social calendar was to fill up, Naomi and I drove north along the coast to Muir Beach, near Muir Woods. There we made our way slowly over the sand to the water, absorbing the elemental energies that converge where ocean meets land. My joy at being in such lovely surroundings was mixed with sadness as we watched children playing on the sandy shore and shouting with glee, for I felt such sympathy for Naomi, having to clutch my arm while she labored to move her almost dead left leg. We sat on the beach together, and when after a while I decided to do a painting, she said, "I'll stay in the car. I can draw and read there." We went back to the car, where I gathered my supplies and then set off, while she got comfortable in the backseat with her sketch pad and books.

I chose a view of the beach from a field studded with wildflowers, and began painting. As happens sometimes, in a couple of hours I found that I did not like my composition, so I scraped it out and returned to the car. There Naomi was working on an intricate drawing—a grid of perhaps thirty small squares, each containing a very different face. Accustomed to her drawings of heads, I adored seeing the variety of finely drawn faces that came from her pen. As usual, the details were exquisite. It seemed that each face was expressing a unique facet of life, and together they were mapping the human soul.

My father-in-law Charles is a tall man, with a full head of gray hair and a long face that shows creases on his brow from years of analyzing problems. He maintains an athletic exuberance for life, and I had always enjoyed being with him because of his passion for good conversation and his ideas for fun excursions. His Jewish faith is much a fact of his existence, although he and Mary rarely attend synagogue.

Since Charles and Mary had stayed abreast of Naomi's struggle, they were prepared to see her limping. Now whenever we went out, Naomi held on to either my arm or her grandpa's. One night when we went out to dinner, Charles commented that Naomi had a "remarkable" spirit. Privately he told me, "It's obvious that she has great difficulty, yet she is so interested in everything!"

On the third day of their visit, I picked up Maria at the airport and drove her to the Seal Rock Inn. She and Naomi hugged, glad to be together again. After a while, Maria and I walked across the street to Sutro Park, where she recounted her godmother Jane's remarkable recovery from cancer after working with Andrei, and asserted, "If anyone can make it, Naomi can. She's so strong!" Returning to the hotel, we picked up Naomi and set off for her daily appointment with Andrei.

We arrived a few minutes early, and as we waited outside the door, a casually dressed middle-aged man ambled up the steps and joined us. Looking surprised, he asked, "What time is your appointment?"

"Two-thirty," I replied. "And yours?"

"I thought mine was two-thirty. Perhaps I'm wrong." He went on to explain that he was a student of Andrei's and had been studying with him for six years. "Andrei's *very* special," he remarked, a glimmer in his eyes.

"What makes him so special?" I asked.

The man tapped a finger on his head, saying, "It's all up here. Very few have developed their mental powers as he has."

Certainly, Andrei had achieved some renown for his curative abilities. While in Santa Barbara, Naomi and I met someone who by coincidence, was trying to get an appointment with him. I discovered also that the manager at the Seal Rock Inn worked in the healing community and knew of Andrei's great reputation. She had even guessed that we were seeing him. Then there was Maria's godmother, Jane, whom Andrei had healed, as well as Jane's friend with cancer.

Suddenly the door swung open and a woman appeared, striding past us down the stairs. A moment later, Andrei confirmed that our appointment for 2:30 was correct, so we said good-bye to the gentleman outdoors and went inside. I introduced Maria as Naomi's friend and soon-to-be assistant. Andrei began by asking Naomi for observations since her previous visit. She replied that she had been a bit tired and her leg now hurt in several places. Andrei hummed, "Good, good," and then clicked on the music and proceeded to work, while Maria and I watched. Fifteen minutes later, he looked at Naomi and said, "Keep observe."

That night Charles and Mary took us all to dinner and a play. The girls were dressed up—Naomi in a black evening dress, and Maria in a brown sleeveless gown. They wore makeup, obviously enjoying their sophistication and a night on the town. After the play, we all went back to the Fairmont together so the girls could see the spectacular view of the city from the Tobiases' suite on the twenty-fifth floor. A corner of their room was entirely glass, affording 180-degree views of the Oakland Bay Bridge and San Francisco, glistening with lights and traffic. Naomi said to Maria, "Isn't that incredible?" We all stood gazing out at the city for a while and then, sharing hugs and kisses and realizing our time together had been special, said good-bye. No one knew it would be a last farewell.

The next morning, Maria and Naomi drove with me to the airport. Before catching my flight to Santa Fe, I kissed Naomi good-bye, and said, "I love you!"

She replied, "I love you, too!"

Maria then added, "Don't worry, I'll take good care of her."

Handing her the keys and swallowing hard to keep down the knot in my throat, I looked into Maria's eyes and thanked her.

Jean met me at the airport in Albuquerque, and as I drove home we updated each other on events there and in San Francisco. After about an hour on the road, we pulled into the driveway. Our two Australian shepherds, Chaco and Sophie, ran up to the car barking, and as I opened the door, Sophie jumped up and stuck her wet nose in my face. A moment later Sarah came out, yelling, "Daddy! You're home!"

Now in the sixth grade, Sarah was turning into a beautiful young woman with brunette hair, round blue-green eyes, and a graceful dancer's form. Under the watchful eyes of her mother, her days were full, with school, homework, dance lessons, violin practice, counseling sessions, and good friendships. Although the weight of her sister's illness sometimes caused her to break down crying, I was glad to know there was always someone she could turn to for comfort.

How good it felt to be home! Waiting for me were chores and responsibilities that reminded me of my former existence, lightening the weight on my heart, if ever so little. The grass needed cutting, our aluminum storage shed had blown over in a heavy wind, letters and bills were stacked on my desk, an easel at the studio I rented in town held an unpainted canvas, and my gallery had scheduled a show for me in July, two months away. Yet the seriousness of our predicament was ever present. While checking my E-mail, I opened a letter from my father, in which he questioned the wisdom of leaving Naomi in San Francisco without an adult. I answered that the two young women were very responsible and would be okay until I returned. Fortunately, I had an appointment scheduled with Arden before the end of the week.

The next day, we had a small birthday celebration. Before blowing out the candles on the cake, I closed my eyes and wished for Naomi's health to be restored. Throughout the day, relatives had called with well wishes, but the one I wanted to hear from most had not, and I was heartsick. Finally, about 9:00 P.M., when I had given up hope of hearing from her, Naomi phoned and said, "Happy birthday, Dad!" When I asked her how things were going, she replied, "Good," her typical euphemism for "enough said."

A few days later I took a long hike in the mountains with Jean and

Sarah, relishing being in the rugged hills of Santa Fe, in clean air at an elevation of 7,000 feet, and among the piñon trees. Nature resurrected my weary spirit. I also began reading a book titled *The Dawnbreakers: Nabíl's Narrative of the Early Days of the Bahá'í Revelation,* where the steadfast and erudite Nabíl chronicles a time that Bahá'ís call the heroic age, when the new religion came under unrelenting persecution by foes determined to eradicate it before it spread. Nabíl, a living witness to this turbulence, recorded how these holy men and women, rather than cowering before their executioners, had gone willingly, often joyfully to their martyrdom, helping to create the dawn of a new age. As I read of their tribulations, I sought to buttress my soul by realizing the positive, even redemptive quality of sacrificial suffering.

Naomi had inspired me to be compassionate and to care for every soul anywhere that had been ruthlessly turned upon by the world. My sense of light and dark had sharpened, and I could see that great souls invariably attract the fiercest opposition. Because of Naomi's endurance of affliction, my heart became sensitive to others who bore hardships, humbling me before their glory. Moreover, Naomi was teaching me the preciousness of life as never before. Her features, the look in her eyes that said, "I am; this is me!" as well as her writing, her art, what she noticed in the world, and the potential of what she might become, were irreplaceable. Just as every human fingerprint is unique, so too, every person makes an imprint in life that is entirely their own. I came to see the preciousness of every person, their awesome importance, the place they hold as a special thread woven into the fabric of humanity. Now upon hearing of a life threatened or lost, I grieved, knowing with respectful sorrow that it could not be replaced.

As the weekend approached, I began to worry about the girls having to switch between the Great Highway Motor Inn and the Seal Rock Inn, so I phoned Naomi. I was surprised to learn that they had moved to the White Cloud Zen Center, which Naomi and I had driven past a few Sundays before and where Maria's godmother, Jane, had lived while seeing Andrei. Meanwhile, my father had put me on edge with his concerns, and I told him that I was in a no-win situation, suffering with Naomi and also suffering away from her. For despite my being with her for over two years now and consecrated to her healing, she was not better but worse, which crushed my heart.

On Sunday afternoon, Maria called her mother Ruth and expressed great anxiety. It had been a difficult day—moving to the Zen center, seeing Naomi in pain during a troublesome delay in getting her prescriptions, and enduring a traffic jam on the Golden Gate Bridge. Ruth suddenly became concerned, and not wanting to burden me in my exhausted state, she talked with Jean and then spoke with my mother, father, and Ann Brode in Santa Barbara. Ruth's call confirmed my father's worries, and immediately he launched a search for an adult willing to go to San Francisco. The last to find out about all this, I felt frustrated and alarmed by the mounting sense of worry being expressed—culminating in the fear, voiced more than once, that Naomi had tried to commit suicide and might try again if Andrei would not see her anymore.

The following day Naomi called to say that Andrei had decided to continue seeing her, and I was overjoyed. Then she added, "But he is making me stop everything else—the cartilage, thymus, vitamins, even the Chi-Lel. It's written in the contract he has given me."

She had invested so much in her daily practice, I could not imagine her quitting suddenly. Yet I knew Naomi was prepared to make the leap; she had always been willing to trust that she could be healed. I asked her how it was going at the Zen center and again, in her sparse way, she answered, "Fine." Then she added, "Don't worry, Dad. Okay?"

To quell my fears and bolster my hopes for a miraculous recovery, I quizzed Ruth, who knew more about Andrei. "Well, he is a physicist, and I know that doctors work with him and study with him. He somehow changes the DNA," she said. Then she told me that Jane's liver had always been small and sickly, but by the end of Andrei's treatments, it had become healthy and normal.

Just such a miracle was what we hoped for with Naomi, because time appeared to be running out. No one wanted to lose her, and it seemed all eyes were upon her as she struggled against a relentlessly powerful opponent.

A PLACE TO LIVE

My life is in God's hands. If He decides it is my time to leave, well then, that is His choice. What I want God to know is that I truly love this earth.

In the course of my second week in Santa Fe, it occurred to me that Kathleen and I had to stand together as Naomi's mother and father, and make peace with ourselves and God. I thought that if anything hidden or unfinished in our relationship could create distress or hardship in the world, it needed to be corrected, at least symbolically. Consequently, one evening I visited Kathleen at her apartment. Together, we looked at our past, made amends, and prayed. We talked about how Naomi was bonded to both of us, and how our separation and divorce must have hurt her as an innocent, trusting child. Then Kathleen prayed with me, asking God's forgiveness. As I got up to leave with tears in my eyes, we hugged, and Kathleen said, "Steven, my medication makes me unable to cry, but

I am crying inside!" With a look of anguish she added, "I want to see Naomi. My cousin has offered to pay for the trip."

"Soon we will have an apartment in San Francisco, and then you can visit," I told her.

During my next session with Arden Fisk, I talked about the issues that were disturbing me most. Every morning, I woke up feeling an ache in my heart and a sense that I was living in a world whose pleasures were merely illusion. Things that seemed to delight people hardly mattered to me. And something else plagued me—what if I had hurt Naomi's chances of recovery by causing a delay in her treatment in Dallas? Dr. Breva had said the delay was "regrettable," and when scans showed the cancer had returned to her lungs, Naomi also had wondered about the impact of our delay. I ached thinking that my overconfidence could actually have hurt her. Arden gazed at me thoughtfully, then asked, "Do you think that if God wanted to cure Naomi, one month would matter? There was no evidence of cancer in her lungs at the end of that month. You are too hard on yourself; whatever you did, you did out of love. You have been right *there* for her, Steven." Then, suggesting my anxiety would be helped by visiting a doctor while in San Francisco, he offered to contact a psychiatrist he knew in the Bay Area. He also advised me to consider taking medication for relief from my intense emotions.

I felt thankful for Arden's encouragement, and after leaving his office I resumed thinking about the matter of choice and consequence. Well, I asked myself, and how does God feel, with dominion over creation while letting his creatures suffer terribly from all manner of afflictions, even creating beings with abnormalities and terrible inherited weaknesses who die painfully? After all, the world is in His All-Powerful hands. Who else can create a human being? Why should I hold myself so accountable? This perspective relieved me of the harsh feelings I directed to myself, allowing for my imperfections since the Perfect Being was above all. Eventually, I came to realize that God dearly loves the afflicted ones, and holds them closely. Because they are so cherished by Him, I concluded, they deserve the utmost consideration from others. At times I envisioned a special recompense awaiting them in the imperishable realm.

As I lay in bed that night contemplating, I recognized that we are *all* touched by chaos, some more obviously than others. Chaos, I decided, plays the role of trickster in our world; it keeps us honest while we search for truth. Without chaos, progress would be meaningless, because progress depends on bringing order from the disorderly place of chaos. But beyond the veils of this worldly struggle stands Eternal God, who watches over all.

A few days later my father's quest, with the help of Ann Brode, proved fruitful. Jill Martin, the photographer from Santa Barbara, had agreed to spend a weekend with Naomi and Maria, providing an adult presence. In addition, he extended a business trip, making an overnight stop in San Francisco for a short visit with the two girls at the Zen center. There he spoke frankly with them, and said he thought that more help was needed. Maria seemed relieved, and after some hesitation, Naomi agreed to the idea. But only after learning that Jill had offered to come was she at ease with it.

When Jill arrived, she introduced Naomi to her young women friends, Julie and Diane, who lived in the city. Julie took Naomi to karaoke parties and sometimes to a group that gathered to do crafts together. Also, Diane and Naomi became friends, sharing an interest in film and going to movies together.

Later, Jill wrote the following about her visit:

> I went to San Francisco with some trepidation, not knowing what state I would find Naomi in. Based on what I had been told about the progression of her illness. I was expecting her to be exhausted from shuffling around a big, unknown city. Instead, I found her to be living her life, trying to make the best of every moment, constantly shifting the focus away from her pain and onto the details of life. She had already made friends at the Zen center,

which is a beautiful place, and she enjoyed showing me a book of photos revealing how it had been built without hardware, always appreciating the details.

That weekend, friends were visiting from Santa Fe and Oregon. While I searched for housing, she went off to Muir Woods and to see the Star Wars movie, The Phantom Menace. *We ate at outdoor cafés and went shoe shopping on Haight Street. We also went to Mel's Drive-In, where we played oldies on the jukebox and sang along.*

When I returned to San Francisco, the girls' time at the Zen center had run out and they had moved back to the Great Highway Motor Inn. Within a few days, everyone had gone home, leaving Naomi and me to continue on our journey together.

Our next mission was to search for an apartment or house to rent until Andrei finished treatments, which could have been months. Staying at the Seal Rock Inn was too expensive long term, and having to move out on weekends was uncomfortable. Naomi's leg remained swollen and painful, sometimes keeping her up at night. Seeing how terrible it looked, I thought: What if she gets gangrene? What if her leg needs to be cut off? Desperation led my mind into loneliness. Sometimes it occurred to me that she would die soon, and become an assisting angel to me. But I would immediately discontinue this line of thinking, because I could not bear the thought of her death. Although my despair still led me at times to wonder why God was allowing her suffering, each night before retiring, Naomi and I prayed together. We prayed for friends and relatives who were ill, reciting Bahá'í prayers for healing. We prayed the Long Healing Prayer, which takes about ten minutes, and also the Short Healing Prayer, which reads as follows:

Thy Name is my healing O Lord, and remembrance of Thee is my remedy. Nearness to Thee is my hope, and love for Thee is my companion. Thy mercy to me is my healing and my succor in both this world and the world to come. Thou, verily, art the All-Bountiful, the All-Knowing, the All-Wise. [1]

Meanwhile, Naomi faithfully complied with Andrei's demand to stop all alternative therapies. As usual, she put her whole self behind the effort of her healer, investing her trust in him. A sack of vitamins, minerals, and herbs stayed untouched, and she had stopped her practice of Chi-Lel. She continued thinking positively and wrote notes to God, such as this one:

Dear God,

I ask that everything I have put into my body today—spiritually and physically—be used to nurture, heal, cure, and strengthen my body completely.

I ask that these gifts I give to my body cause it to feel the beauty, bounty, and wholeness of life. I know that my body welcomes these good things.

I also know that my body is wise enough to recognize cancer and get rid of it completely.

I see my body as a strong giver of life!

We remained hopeful about Andrei's treatments, and when again I broached the subject of payment, he once more told me "no." His refusal to accept money added to the mystery that surrounded him, especially as I had learned that he was normally quite expensive.

Then one day he really surprised us by telling us to go home, get scans, and let him continue to work with Naomi over the phone. Unable to fathom how we could leave with Naomi in this condition, I replied, "We are looking for an apartment, and plan to live in San Francisco now."

"But that is too expensive," he said. "Go home and call me."

Stunned, I answered, "We will get scans here and find an apartment to live in. We want to stay; it is too hard to go back now."

Exasperated, he shrugged his huge shoulders and turned away to write something in his book. Facing me again, he handed over a paper with the next appointment on it. "Good-bye," he said.

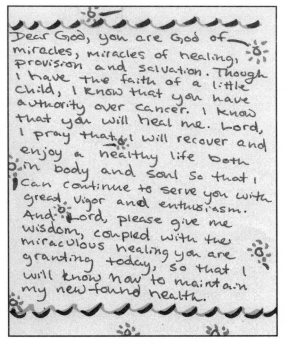

One of Naomi's notes to God

Soon I noticed an advertisement in the paper for a short-term rental of a two-bedroom house and made an appointment to look at it. Driving to the Bernal Heights district of San Francisco, we arrived at a two-story house on a short, sloping street called Shotwell. Naomi held on to my arm as we approached the front door and rang the doorbell. We heard barking from inside, then the door swung open and a short woman with curly blonde hair and a round cherub face stood smiling with two dogs at her heels. "Hello, I'm Michelle," she said. "Please come in."

We walked down the hall to a room that served as a kitchen, eating area, and living room, with a breathtaking view of the city. The windows were open, and the space was light and airy. Michelle introduced us to her husband Tony and eleven-year-old stepdaughter Robin, and before long we were sipping cold drinks and getting to know one another. Michelle was a physician, practicing internal medicine at a nearby hospital, while Tony, a carpenter, managed their two other properties, and enjoyed sailing whenever possible. They were going to visit Michelle's family in Florida for several months and wanted to rent their house. I told them about our situation, briefly describing Naomi's illness and what we had been through over the last two years. Then Tony showed me on a map the quickest way to Andrei's house, guessing it would take about twenty minutes. We thanked them, promised to stay in touch, and then set out on a trial run to Andrei's following the course Tony had drawn. The drive, requiring a fair amount of zigzagging up and down through busy neighborhoods, did indeed take about twenty minutes—twice as long as we had been accustomed to.

Naomi liked the feeling of the Bernal Heights house. She could sleep in Robin's room on the entry level, using a bathroom directly across the hall; I could stay in the master bedroom upstairs; and there was plenty of room for visitors. Tony had even offered to put up handicap railing by the bathtub. Agreeing that we could be comfortable there, we called Michelle back that evening to confirm that we would move in the following week.

Next, we had to find an oncologist in the area, and by coincidence, we learned that Jill's friend Diane had a sister, Krista Muirhead, who worked as a pediatric oncologist in San Rafael, a small community twenty minutes north of the Golden Gate Bridge. Diane mentioned that their mother had died of cancer, which had inspired Krista to study oncology. When Naomi and I met her at the hospital, she greeted us with a warm smile and showed us to an examining room. Dressed in a white coat, she was of medium height, with attentive green eyes and reddish auburn hair. After examining Naomi and briefly discussing our situation, she promised to be in touch with Dr. Hodder in Santa Barbara and to begin scheduling the scans. Then she gave us a prescription for more pain patches, and we left for the Seal Rock Inn, tooting our horn in the tunnel before the Golden Gate Bridge.

By this time Naomi was going to bed at night with mounds of pillows under her leg. Comfort did not come easily, nor did sleep, yet each morning she got up, dressed, and usually went with me to the nearby coffee shop, where she drank tea and nibbled on a bagel. Mornings were the hardest time for her to keep food down.

As usual, we kept busy. Some days we visited museums, where I would push Naomi around in a wheelchair as we discussed the artwork. At the California Palace of the Legion of Honor Museum, we studied the Renaissance art with its moving depictions of the life and death of Jesus Christ, a popular motif in Europe between the fourteenth and seventeenth centuries. Renaissance means rebirth, and the artists of the time sought to portray heaven, hell, suffering, hope, love, and salvation. In one room, we were drawn to an exquisitely crafted late-sixteenth-century German wooden cabinet that had taken a master craftsman many months to create. Set on a broad pedestal, it just reached Naomi's eye level, so she was able to delight in the artist's painstaking carving and millwork while sitting in her wheelchair. Probably a commission from a wealthy nobleman, the piece was inlaid with exotic woods to portray hunting scenes on the outside panels, which opened to reveal many drawers, each with its own scene, many of which were biblical. Naomi gleefully pointed out different facets of the magical box; its life seemed inexhaustible, and every drawer beckoned her to wonder what treasure it had held. I attributed Naomi's fascination to the scenes of hunters and hunted, to saints offering salvation, and to the mysteries hidden behind the closed doors—all elements of her current life.

On another day, we went to the Exploratorium in San Francisco, walking slowly through all the exhibits arm in arm. Here many interactive displays offered hands-on experiences relating to physical science, and Naomi wanted to stop at each one. Ordinarily I would not have had the patience, but she was happy, so we stayed until closing. Her enthusiasm showed she was still eager for new experiences and had a voracious appetite for living. She embraced each opportunity with a joyful heart, relishing life's wonder and beauty as a salve to her pain.

Barbara Miller, Naomi's longtime Waldorf school teacher, offered to come and stay for five days beginning June 4, the day after our move to the house on Shotwell, so that I could return to Santa Fe. Since the two had maintained a close camaraderie over the years, Naomi called her Barbara instead of Mrs. Miller. The mother of four grown children, Barbara was married to Preston Miller, a Waldorf school teacher turned massage therapist. The two of them had met while Preston was teaching at the Santa Fe Waldorf School; then they married and combined families. Several years later, while Preston and his son Leander, age fourteen, were hiking in the mountains of Colorado, Leander fell from a cliff and died instantly. After carrying his dead son down the mountain alone, Preston went through years of grieving. Barbara knew the terrain.

Arranging for her arrival, Barbara and a good friend named Dee, who lived in the Bay Area, agreed to meet Naomi and me at the old windmill in the Golden Gate Park. I planned to leave the following day.

On June 4, we packed our belongings to leave the Seal Rock Inn for the last time. During our stays there, we had come to recognize almost all the staff, and they had come to know us—the man, and the young woman who limped, always arm-in-arm together. Most of them knew of our circumstances from Cecilia, the manager, with whom I had become friends. After saying our farewells, we went to an appointment at Andrei's, and then drove to the Golden Gate Park to wait for Barbara and Dee at the gardens by the windmill.

It was a balmy, clear day with only a few fluffy white clouds. Earlier, when we had arrived in San Francisco, the flower beds around the windmill had been alive with masses of radiant tulips and poppies. Now they were replaced by foxgloves, begonias, and other flowers adorning the neat beds adjacent to the lawn, making us aware of the passage of time. We walked slowly and carefully arm-in-arm down the footpath to admire the flowers, and then turned to find a seat on a bench by the windmill.

As we sat admiring the manicured gardens and talking, Barbara, Dee, and Dee's dog arrived. Barbara gave Naomi a kiss and said, "This is Dee. She is a nurse, and we've been friends forever. She used to live in Santa Fe. She can tell you all sorts of stories about people who have beaten cancer."

Dee, slightly heavy with a mass of graying, dark, curly hair tied back behind her head, immediately hit it off with Naomi. After talking a while, we said good-bye to Dee and headed to the house on Shotwell.

When we arrived, Tony and Michelle were scrambling to get the house in order and leave on their trip. Robin gave Naomi a huge scroll and, with a shy smile, said, "This is from my class." We unrolled it, and to our surprise, the entire fifth grade had written notes of love and encouragement. It was an unexpected display of affection that touched us. Though never having met Naomi, the teacher and kids had decided to openly support her in her struggle. Michelle had bought fresh-cut flowers for the house, and Tony had installed a new washer and dryer as well as the bathtub railing for Naomi.

That evening Barbara fell asleep on Naomi's bed while Tony and Michelle were finishing their packing upstairs. After they left, Naomi went to bathe and I read a book. Soon Naomi stepped out of the bathroom wrapped in a towel, her hair wet, and in a shaky voice, said, "Dad, I have been avoiding looking at myself. But after my bath, I glanced in the mirror, and now I am really upset. Look!" She unwrapped her towel and stood naked in front of me. Her left hip was badly misshapen, with a lump at its crest, and her leg very swollen. "Look at this," she exclaimed, pointing to a big blue vein protruding two inches below her navel. "I need to have faith in Andrei," she said, nearly crying. "He doesn't tell me anything. I need to have faith in him." Shaken, I replied that maybe she should open up to him with her concerns, express herself, and ask him the difficult questions that troubled her. She groaned to herself, and went back into the bathroom, shutting the door behind her. I felt hope slipping away, and my heart ached, *as if an arrow sent from an unseen hand had found its mark deep within my heart.*

In anguish, I woke Barbara and told her what had just happened, sharing my despair. After talking a while, we both agreed that Naomi had great strength and was deeply loved. Furthermore, we were doing everything we could and not giving up.

That night I barely slept. Lying in bed, I thought about Naomi's disfigurement and the big vein. Might it be bulging because of the strain of supplying so much blood to the growing cancer? I shuddered at the thought and got up to smoke a cigarette. Back in bed, tossing restlessly, I asked, "Where are you, God? Why are you letting this hideous disfigurement injure Naomi?" Although I tried, I could not shake the anxiety caused by Naomi's pain, yet deep within I knew, like Mary, mother of Jesus, that great suffering borne for the love of God was the highest redemption possible, and that she was safe.

Moreover, I knew that at a time when He was imprisoned and beset with sorrow at the darkness of the world, Bahá'u'lláh wrote the *Fire Tablet,* in which He essentially asks God, like I now was: Where is your might, your glory, and evidence of your power? After many such entreaties, God replies with these encouraging words:

> *Were it not for calamity, how would the sun of Thy patience shine, O Light of the worlds?* [2]

I kept my faith, as did Naomi, clinging to the Heavenly Father, and yet my aching was deep, like my love. I saw Naomi's life shining and could not think of losing her. I recalled her words, uttered only a few days before: "Something I could live for is to share an inner wisdom I have—to assist others to heal." I prayed for God to protect her. Finally, I dozed a few hours before going to the airport for my flight to Albuquerque.

FIRE TESTS THE GOLD

**I realize that thoughts are not 100 percent pure and good,
but I sure do hate it when they are negative.**

In Santa Fe, despite taking walks with Jean and Sarah, and working in the garden and at my studio, I was preoccupied with thoughts of Naomi. Every morning, I woke with a dull, aching sadness in my heart that left me almost unable to move. Forcing myself to get up, I would regain composure and slowly begin to function. I was not praying for healing as much now, feeling that my supplications to save Naomi were useless, and that God had His own plan and would protect her. The part of me that wanted victory began firming up for disappointment, realizing more deeply than before that the world is merely a testing place for our souls. As for my soul, I felt, as is written in the *Bhagavad-Gita:*

Not this world's kingdom,
Supreme, unchallenged,
No, nor the throne
Of the gods in heaven,
Could ease this sorrow
That numbs my senses! [1]

One day at the gallery, I was alone talking with Freshtah, a Persian Bahá'í friend who who worked there. She had lived in Iran with her husband, Saifi, but left with him because of persecution. Her family had been praying for Naomi, and now Freshtah asked how things were. I searched for the right words, first saying, "Well, she is strong but . . . " Finally I cried out, "She is dying." Freshtah began to weep. Then after gathering some composure, I remarked that although Naomi had become stronger, her illness had gained strength as well. "It seems the stronger Naomi becomes, the worse it gets for her," I added, thinking, *the heat is being turned up now for the gold to purify.*

In San Francisco, Barbara struggled with Naomi's terrible condition. Because Naomi could not get comfortable in bed, she got up at night. Barbara, hearing her, did not sleep well, feeling the helplessness that was the curse of all those who loved Naomi.

During the days, after appointments with Andrei the two visited Dee, went to the park, to movies, ate out, and talked about mutual friends. Together they went to Kaiser Permanente Hospital in San Rafael for the X rays of Naomi's lungs that Dr. Muirhead had ordered. One evening, they went to Oakland for dinner at Dee's house. Dee's husband Saumitra, from India, had to carry Naomi up the front steps and into the house. The two of them struck an immediate rapport, especially since both Naomi and Saumitra had something personal in common: their mothers were mentally ill. Later, after Naomi choked on some tea and threw up, Saumitra took her soiled clothes to the laundry. Soon after, Barbara went into the kitchen to talk with Dee. As Naomi sat in the living room reading, she soon heard the two friends talking about her, and called out, "Barbara, will you come here a minute?" Barbara looked at her as if to say, "Uh-oh, I'm in trouble now!" Naomi stated she wanted to be sure her condition was *not* a topic for conversation.

The day before Barbara left, Naomi's friends Mira and Travis arrived from Eugene to help out for four days. Mira was in school at the University of Oregon, and Travis worked as a carpenter. Each about the same height, Mira had golden-brown curly locks encircling her broad face, and Travis was relaxed, easygoing, and perceptive.

When Naomi didn't have appointments with Andrei, the three engaged in enjoyable activities such as motorboating on the lake at the Golden Gate Park and taking a sunset voyage aboard a charter sailing ship on the bay. The bay can be chilly and cold in the evening, so during the sail they ended up huddling under blankets. But amidst all the activity, Naomi had forgotten to change her Duragesic patch, and unfortunately, Mira and Travis witnessed the agony that always dwelled just beneath the surface of her life.

About this time, I was at Arden's office in Santa Fe, trying to face the big picture. I told him that I knew God was close to us and we were devoted to Him, so why did He allow such gruesome events to befall us? I had depended on God and miracles, but miracles were not forthcoming. How could I live thinking there was no hope for Naomi? I knew I could not be angry or frustrated with God, the All-Wise, since my problems stemmed from my limited understanding of divine reality. Further, I felt that I was falling short of the noble examples set by others of my faith, particularly `Abdu'l-Baha', who since childhood was known as one who greeted every trial no matter how severe with the same patient equanimity. Arden, however, made a clear distinction, and said that `Abdúl-Bahá had a different personality and was a particularly elevated and wise soul whom I should not compare myself with. "Your precious, beloved daughter is being ripped apart in front of your very eyes. It is understandable that you feel terrible anguish," he reassured me. In truth, many times I felt abandoned and cried out in misery to the universe, wanting to pummel the earth with my fists. Alone in my studio, I smashed long, thick, cardboard tubes against the walls and concrete floor in anger and despair. I did not understand Bahá'u'lláh's admonition to "be not among those who are sorely agitated." My obsessive-compulsive tendencies were flaring up, and repeatedly I thought I could make everything right for Naomi. But I could not, which was unacceptable to me, so my thought pattern would begin over again in a vicious circle. Arden advised me again to contact his psychiatrist friend in San Francisco for support.

Then one morning we received a surprise call from a stranger, who said, "Hello, Mr. Boone, this is Sarah McCarthy from Westwind Travel. I don't quite know how to put this, and you don't need to answer me right this minute, but an anonymous couple would like to pay for your daughter Naomi to take a trip with a friend anywhere in the world!"

I thanked her for this remarkably kind gesture, and said, "Please convey our deep gratitude and let the people know that I will pass the message along to Naomi. She is being treated in San Francisco right now."

When I told Naomi, she was equally surprised, and guessed that the trip had been offered by our neighbors.

As the days passed, Naomi worried even more about her health, and wrote the following touching note that began with a quotation from Bahá'u'lláh:

> *Be patient under all conditions and put your whole trust and confidence in God.* [2]

> *Oh God, I am upset. I just don't know what to do! Should I continue to work with Andrei? Should I use my two round-trip tickets to go on a trip? Should I pursue the advanced clinical trials*

program that Grandpa told me about at UCLA? What should I do? At this time, I don't feel like Andrei is making me better. Since working with him, my walking, the pain, the swelling, and my lungs all feel worse! I am scared; I don't know what to do. I just want to live!

On June 13, I returned to San Francisco with Kathleen, who was scheduled to stay until June 18. Jean and Sarah planned to arrive on June 17. When Kathleen and I entered the house on Shotwell, Naomi, Mira, and Travis were lounging in the living room. They seemed contented and happy, but I could not help noticing Naomi's thin body. Her face had become taut, revealing her beautiful high cheekbones, and accentuating her round eyes like lakes ablaze in shimmering moonlight. Kathleen greeted her warmly, and Naomi threw an arm forward to give her mother a hug, introduced Mira and Travis, and suggested seeing a movie. Looking in the paper, we noticed that a new Austin Powers comedy, *The Shag*, was playing at a theater downtown, and we decided to go see it. Driving into the city, I was lucky to find a parking place a block from the theater entrance. With Mira and Travis ahead of us, Kathleen and I walked slowly alongside Naomi up the steep sidewalk to the theater. Looking straight ahead, Naomi suddenly asked, "Dad, how does my walking seem to you?"

"It seems you are doing well," I replied, having sensed that she was somehow stronger.

"It seems worse to me," she said, still staring. "Are you sure?"

I was telling the truth when I said she seemed stronger, but what I was perceiving was her gloriously dancing spirit, in the last dazzling flames of her life. For she already had a foot in the other world.

When we arrived at the theater, the lobby was packed with people waiting in long lines for tickets. Slowly shuffling forward, we finally reached the ticket counter, and learned to our dismay that the movie was sold out. So we bought tickets for an adventure-horror flick called *The Mummy*. I did not want to see a horror movie, or subject Naomi to one, and Kathleen was hesitant, but the youngsters wanted to try it. Unfortunately, although the action and special effects were thrilling, the film glorified pain and torture, which was hard to endure sitting next to someone whose pain and torture were real.

The next day Mira and Travis left, and Kathleen spent more time with Naomi, commenting to me that she seemed better. Kathleen told her, "I know you are going to go to college and will live to be at least fifty!" Then at Andrei's the following day, Kathleen spoke up and asked him, "Do you think she is going to live a long time?" Andrei seemed taken aback and answered, "I'm working on it."

But then the next morning as we stood talking, Kathleen admitted that she did not know if Naomi would live, and said, "Naomi told me, 'Life is unfair.' My mother died of cancer, and at times she also said life is not fair." Later admitting that the mental illness had plagued her, Kathleen thanked me for being with our daughter throughout the ordeal, telling me, "I could not have done it."

We tried to get the new X rays from Kaiser Permanente Hospital in San Rafael, but Dr. Muirhead was away and the accompanying report could not be located. We did, however, leave with another prescription for pain medicine—an increased dosage since Naomi complained that she was hurting more.

Soon Jean and Sarah arrived in San Francisco, and Kathleen left. I was glad that she had visited Naomi, knowing the love they felt for each other. Every day now, the weather was beautiful and our little family went forth: Andrei's, Legion of Honor Museum, Golden Gate Park, Japanese Tea Garden, and Muir Woods. Jean noticed Naomi's new strength and hoped that Andrei might be healing her. Yet Naomi confided, "It feels like my symptoms are getting worse."

The day we went to the redwood forest Naomi needed a wheelchair, and as I pushed her along I remembered our earlier visit when she had been able to walk. I knew she did not want to be pushed around in a wheelchair and was troubled by her inability to walk. As we finished our stroll, Naomi pointed to the fallen tree we had noticed during our previous visit and said, "Look, Sarah, see how a new tree has grown from the dead one. Isn't that amazing!" Her voice was so full of life that I thought surely a nightingale's song had roused me from a fitful sleep. Inspirational moments like these, in which Naomi reminded me of the powerful beauty of life, made my exhaustion and anxiety vanish.

Jean and I talked about getting a walker that Naomi could hold on to for support. Although she did not like the idea at first, she at last agreed it would be practical. At the medical supply store, a gentleman adjusted one to fit Naomi's height. It unfolded so that she could grasp short rails on either side; and leaning forward, she could push it along, moving the two wheels in front and dragging the two legs in back. Grasping hold of it, Naomi took a few steps, then looked sadly into my eyes and cried for just a moment, two or three tears rolling down her cheeks. Out on the street we tried to be encouraging, as if it were nothing for a young woman to be seen pushing a walker. When we went to a movie that evening, I noticed Naomi had started coughing, and I heard a raspy noise when she breathed, which concerned me.

The following day, Naomi woke up coughing and later threw up her breakfast. We sat with her while she sipped tea, gathering her strength. Then the whole family drove to Andrei's, surprising him by showing up together at his front door. We sat near him as he swirled his arms around Naomi, shaking his hands while the strange music played, and we hoped that he was healing her. As usual, when we left he said, "Good, keep observe." Afterward we crossed Fulton Avenue to the Golden Gate Park, where I painted in a rose garden while Jean and Sarah took Naomi to an appointment with a psychologist she had begun seeing. Then later we all went to Story Lake in the park, where Naomi had had such fun with Mira and Travis that she insisted we go. In the parking lot she pushed her walker slowly, stopping frequently to catch her breath. Reaching the boat landing, we gave the walker to an attendant and climbed on board one of the electric motorboats. Then off we went, slowly gliding around an island in the middle of the lake. Tall trees arched overhead, shading flowering shrubs along the banks underneath. Seagulls perched on our bow, while ducks swam over to get morsels of bread we threw to them. Naomi coughed, but eagerly pointed out flowers and birds, spotting big nests in the treetops. As we cruised back to the landing, she exclaimed, "Wasn't that beautiful!" It had been a special sharing, floating around the lake together in our little boat, all the while captivated by the exquisite surroundings.

That evening we went to the Cliff House restaurant, a century-old landmark establishment at Seal Rock Point that offered dining overlooking the Pacific. When our dinner was served, Naomi ate slowly and carefully, and an elderly woman at another table kept peering over at us intently. Naomi's walker rested by our table; her ninety-five-pound body looked thin and frail. I wondered if the woman sensed somehow that Naomi's time was running out. I resented her staring and tried to ignore it, focusing instead on the sun as it set over the ocean, filling the room with its golden light. For a moment, I thought it odd that the world was still beautiful while my gallant daughter sitting next to me was so near death. At Naomi's request we took a drive after dinner, along the ocean and through some neighborhoods so that Jean and Sarah could see the city houses.

We returned to Kaiser Permanente Hospital the next day. At Jean's prompting, it had been decided to get scans of Naomi's pelvis and leg. Jean supposed Andrei might want to see them too. When I asked Andrei, he replied, "Yes, get them all."

At the hospital, a wheelchair was brought for Naomi, and a nurse ushered us into the waiting area. Inside, the cold air reinforced the chilling feeling that our destiny would soon be revealed from within the bowels of monstrous machinery which moved back and forth over bodies, gazing emotionless at each quivering cell within. Naomi had always disliked scans, and her experience with them today would be the worst yet. Getting her into position within the barrel of the machine was terrible. Then during the first pass, she was in so much pain lying on her back and unable to move, with her swollen leg flat down, that she cried out. After elevating her leg on layers of folded towels, she went back inside for more pictures.

Next, the radiologist, needing more views, asked if she could handle her discomfort a while longer. Visibly very upset, Naomi agreed to try if they could help get her more comfortable. She was being as brave as she could be, but I could tell she was nearing her limit. I gazed at my weakened daughter lying on the scanning track in this cold room, so frail and vulnerable with her painfully swollen leg, in misery, dressed in sweatpants with tennis shoes, and not wanting to think of what the scans would reveal. I remembered when she was a strong runner who loved pounding the earth with her feet, working herself into a sweat, drinking in the air, and feeling the wind blowing through her hair. Afterward, in her tennis shoes and sweatpants, flushed and out of breath, she'd throw an arm around a teammate, and they would laugh joyfully together.

Why had her life been whittled down to this? Feeling such love for my daughter that I could have burst, I thought, she is right—life is not fair. We adjusted more towels under her leg, and back she went into the scanning tube. Finally, just as Naomi cried, "Stop! I can't stand this anymore!" it was over.

Outside, heat rose from the black asphalt parking lot, and the bright sun practically blinded us as we went to the car. We had the previous X rays now, and the report that went with them, which Jean held in a yellow manila folder on her lap. Eager to read the report, she asked, "Don't you want to look at them?" Curse the damn results! I did not want to see them, preferring to hand them directly to Andrei. I dreaded the diagnosis and was angry that our fate might be written on a paper that eventually would be thrown away with so much other trash. "No, I don't want to see them," I answered, pulling to a stop at a red light.

Jean looked over her shoulder at Naomi, who was playing cards with Sarah in the backseat. "Do you want to know the results?"

"Not really," Naomi replied. "Just give them to Andrei."

On the highway, Jean read the report silently, then carefully slid it in its folder without saying a word. To lighten the somber mood as we drove through the tunnel, I honked the horn and yelled, "Yippee!" Naomi and Sarah also yelled, "Yippee," and then they went back to playing cards.

Later, we gave the X rays and report to Andrei, who silently put them aside and then worked on Naomi. Her coughing and the rasp in her breathing had continued, and Andrei asked if mucus was coming up. Perhaps, I thought, this is part of her healing. I wanted to believe and to keep hope alive. As Andrei worked around her with his hands, I watched Naomi's face, noticing concentration and something else—an expression of spiritual tiredness I had never seen before. My heart sank. The fight had left her, which I took as a signal for surrender, indicating our war was over.

When we returned to the house, Naomi called Jill in Santa Barbara. Amazingly, after the painful ordeal at the hospital and my bitter disappointment, I heard her laughing, and thought, how I adore you, my strong one!

THE LIGHT IN THE TUNNEL

God is with me. I just need to give it all to Him.

Before Jean and Sarah were to leave for Santa Fe, Naomi made an appointment to see a manicurist with Sarah at an upscale salon that had been recommended by a friend. The day of their appointment, I drove downtown with the girls, planning to leave them at the salon, which was located in a fancy business district, then go to a bookstore and return for them later. Naomi got out of the car slowly, grabbed on to her walker, and started for the salon about half a block away. I noticed with concern that she tired easily and seemed out of breath, needing to stop and rest every seven feet or so. At last we reached the reception desk, no doubt looking odd amidst the sophisticated clientele—Naomi and Sarah both in tennis shoes and jeans, and Naomi holding on to her walker. Speaking up, she informed the secretary that they had arrived for manicures. The young woman looked at the appointment book and smiled at Naomi, saying, "Right this way!"

Naomi and Sarah, the day of their salon visit

I knew the girls' time together would be special. Giving them hugs, I left, telling them, "Be back in an hour." When I returned, they showed off their beautifully finished fingernails. In the car, I turned around and asked, "Was that fun, Sarah?"

"Uh-huh," she nodded, holding her hands up to gaze admiringly at her shiny red nails. Naomi held her fingers up for me to see and said, "I got a French manicure." Her flawless nails glistened with a clear polish, all the cuticles neat and even.

That weekend we took a trip up the Napa Valley to Calistoga. The region was busy with tourists, since stock car races were being held. We had wanted to spend the night in a hotel, but every one we stopped at was booked. At last we found a hot springs resort with an outdoor swimming pool where we could use the facilities, provided Jean and I booked massages. The spacious pool was up a flight of stairs, and once we unloaded our things, I began helping Naomi with the climb. She tired after only a few steps. Sitting on a bench, her head drooping between her shoulders, she said, "Dad, I did not want to tell you, but ever since my coughing fit last weekend I have not been able to take a full breath." Startled at her deteriorating condition, I lifted her up the stairs on my shoulder and set her in a shaded patio chair by the poolside. Naomi was so fatigued she could not move, so she asked Sarah to get a book out of her swimming bag, and Jean handed her a bottle of water. We looked at the people playing in the pool and sunbathing comfortably in chairs nearby. Were they living in a dream world or were we? Naomi told us to go for our massages, so Jean and I left.

While the masseuse kneaded my back, I thought of Naomi alone by the pool with her book in her lap and unable to get a full breath of air. I recalled how longingly she had looked at the water, and knew her disappointment at being a passive onlooker. Immediately after my massage, I went back to the pool and looked for her, but she was gone. Startled, I searched around quickly and soon spotted her sitting at the children's end of the pool in her bathing suit, with her feet dangling in the water. She sat watching the children play around her, pain patches all over her upper arm and chest, thin and gaunt, her left leg about twice the size of the right one. Despite my sadness at her condition, my heart soared at her indomitable strength. *The warrior has fully emerged.* She was like a boxer in the ring who, bloodied, pummeled, and almost senseless, nonetheless struggles up again to meet the opponent. Her big heart would not quit.

After Jean returned, she also was amazed that Naomi had managed to get in the pool. Then while Jean swam laps, I helped Naomi to a chair, covering her with towels. When it was time to leave, she could not make it down the handicap ramp pushing her walker, and said, "I can't do it, Dad. You have to carry me." Wheelchairs weren't available, so I asked a young spa attendant to help.

Crossing our arms and holding each other's wrists, we made a seat for her and carried her to the car. At the car, he talked with Naomi, and after hearing that she hoped to be starting college in Oakland that fall, he wished her well. It was touching to hear Naomi speak with such hope, but painful to realize the impossibility of her dream.

At times I again feared Naomi's leg would have to be cut off, but I was unable to imagine what good it would do if cancer remained in her lungs. Devastated at such moments, I remembered lines from a prayer by Bahá'u'lláh:

> *The companions of all who adore Thee are the tears they shed, and the comforters of such as seek Thee are the groans they utter, and the food of them who hasten to meet Thee is the fragments of their broken hearts.* [1]

Naomi's life was ablaze and yet she danced on the flames. She was not frightened and continued to find the silver lining in life. Her undertaking is perhaps best described in these stanzas by Chinese poet Shu Ting:

> *You believed in your own story,*
> *then climbed inside it—*
> *a turquoise flower.*
> *You gazed past ailing trees,*
> *past crumbling walls and rusty railings.*
> *Your least gesture beckoned a constellation*
> *of wild vetch, grasshoppers, and stars*
> *to sweep you into immaculate distances.*
>
> *The heart may be tiny*
> *but the world's enormous.*
>
> *And the people in turn believe—*
> *in pine trees after rain,*

ten thousand tiny suns, a mulberry branch
bent over water like a fishing rod,
a cloud tangled in the tail of a kite.
Shaking off dust, in silver voices
ten thousand memories sing from your dream.

The world may be tiny
but the heart's enormous. [2]

Following Arden's advice, I contacted the Bay Area doctor he had suggested for counseling. The day of my appointment, Naomi went with me and sat reading in the car while I entered the apartment building. I climbed a steep, winding staircase to the third floor, where the psychiatrist met me and led me to his office. He looked middle-aged, was dressed impeccably in a brown suit, and had a mild, thoughtful manner. Once we were seated facing each other, I described my situation, and also relayed how Arden had advised me to continue receiving counseling and perhaps even obtain medicine to help relieve my unremitting anxiety. The doctor listened carefully, and at last suggested that a prescription drug called Paxil might help level out my roller-coaster emotions.

Remembering a troubled time in my youth when a psychiatrist had put me on Thorazine, which blocked my feeling life, I said that although my pain over Naomi's condition was extreme, I did not want to block my feelings. To be a cardboard man with no emotions at a time when my beloved daughter was dying would be worse than anxiety and heartbreak. Looking straight into his eyes, I told him, "I cry sometimes, and I need and want to be able to weep. I won't take a drug that will block my grief."

"You will still feel," he replied, "but you'll be more accepting of your feelings."

As he handed me some packets of Paxil, I said I would begin taking one-half the normal dosage. Then I made an appointment to see him in a week.

Soon Tony returned from Florida to take care of some personal matters, and he invited us to go sailing. Naomi wanted to accept Tony's offer for an afternoon excursion on the bay, but she was not strong enough, and Jean wanted us to stay together. With each new activity Naomi could not accept, I despaired more, sensing her decline.

A few days later, as she and I were relaxing in the afternoon sun, she confided her fears, saying, "It seems as though everyone is giving up on me. I can feel people thinking I am going to die." A flood of emotions swept through me as she added, "Oh, Dad, there is so much I want to do! I want to go to college and make new friends. I want to have a boyfriend and get married someday. I want to see Sarah get married, and be at her wedding. I want to travel to places I've never been." Feeling how much I wanted her to have everything she longed for, I sat in silence. Then looking at her, I answered sadly, "I pray that God gives you all the desires of your heart, Naomi." Soon I helped her up, and we inched our way toward the house. Reaching the patio door, she stopped to catch her breath before stepping inside.

That evening, Naomi checked her E-mail, and as usual found many letters from well-wishers. After replying to them all, she closed her laptop. Hours later, when I went to use it, I noticed that she had written herself a note as well, for there in big capital letters on the screen were the words:

GOD IS WITH ME
HEALING ME NOW!
I LOVE YOU, NAOMI.
I BELIEVE IN YOU!!
I AM HEALING NOW.

The next morning as Jean and Sarah prepared to return to Santa Fe, they stood by Naomi's bedside to say good-bye. After everyone shared hugs, Jean kissed Naomi, telling her, "I love you . . . I believe in your strength!" Naomi looked up at her from bed, where she lay with a mountain of pillows under her swollen leg, and replied, "I love you, too."

On the street, I embraced Jean and said good-bye, then kissed Sarah on the head. As they rode off in the airport shuttle, I waved, feeling an ache at their leaving, and then I returned inside. Naomi asked me to get her clothes down from the shelf, so I handed her a pair of blue jeans, a shirt, and socks. She sat up, dangling her legs over the edge of the mattress, and slumping forward to stare at her foot, offhandedly remarked, "Oh, look at my poor foot—it's so swollen!" I was touched by the affection in her voice, and indeed her left foot was so swollen it looked like it might burst. She dressed slowly, while I made tea for her before our appointment with Andrei.

This morning, it seemed that the slightest exertion exhausted her. She could barely move. I suggested canceling our appointment, but she replied, "No, I have to go," and asked me to carry her to the car. The hallway was narrow, however, and I was afraid of hurting her, so instead I helped her step-by-step with the walker until we finally made it outside. On the way to Andrei's she dozed off for minutes at a time. Then when we arrived, she looked at the stairs and said, "You will have to carry me."

Never had I seen her so weak. Feeling that we were in peril and I could no longer care for her by myself, I said, "Naomi, I can't do this on my own anymore. We must go back to Santa Fe." She was silent a few moments, as if coming to terms with my proposal, or perhaps weighing her options, and then said, "All right."

I felt relieved that we could return home while there was still time. But I also felt sad, knowing her deep disappointment, for I had long sensed she had made an inner promise to go home only when she was healthy. Opening her door, I helped get her legs out, lifted her forward so she could stand, then leaned down while she fell over my shoulder. Kicking the car door shut, I carried her up the stairs, thinking that someone seeing us would wonder what had happened to Naomi. Andrei answered the door and watched as I carried her into the living room, put her in the chair, and glanced at him as if to say, "Look at my darling. What has she done to deserve this?" When Andrei began working on Naomi, who sat unsteadily in front of him with her eyes closed, he observed that her condition had deteriorated over the weekend; her head occasionally dropped onto her chest, then jerked back up. And as I watched, I began sobbing uncontrollably. "What are we going to do?" I cried.

"This is why I told you, go home!" he said. "You have your doctors there, and I can work on her from here."

"No, we don't have doctors there! The doctors were in Dallas," I replied in despair. He looked surprised, and then I told him we were going home to Santa Fe as soon as possible.

Right now, however, it was obvious that we needed to go to an emergency room since Naomi was not getting enough oxygen. I told Andrei I had to get her to a hospital very soon. And as he stood beside her, arms at his side, I realized he had tried with all his power to help Naomi during the many hours we had spent with him. "Please, I must pay you something," I said.

Again he refused, saying, "No, not necessary."

Then Naomi asked in a weak voice if she could call him from Santa Fe, and he replied, "Yes."

When I had gotten Naomi back out to the car, I decided to drive the twenty minutes to Kaiser Permanente Hospital because her records were there. On the way across town she seemed to slip in and out of consciousness. One moment she would be talking with me, and the next she would be silent, her head on her chest.

As we approached the bridge, she perked up momentarily. "Dad, I had a dream a while ago: *You carried me up the stairs at Andrei's and there was a wedding with many people, including you and Andrei.* Was it my wedding?" she asked, her voice trailing off, her chin sinking back down on her chest. I realized in amazement that her dream foretold her nuptials to the Lord. I pictured carrying her up the stairs as I had just done, a happy crowd at the top rejoicing for her, with Andrei there. "But what a difference between the splendor of the image Naomi has just described and our present circumstance," I remarked silently to myself, driving through drizzling rain toward the hospital. As we crossed the bridge, the sky was overcast, with only bits of blue showing through. Naomi looked up to see where we were, and then her head slumped forward again. She needs oxygen desperately, I thought, heading toward the tunnel. Upon entering the dark recess, I began calculating how long it would take to get to the hospital when all of a sudden I heard a soft, "Yippee!"

Startled, I looked over at Naomi, who then asked in a weak voice, "Dad, aren't you going to honk the horn?"

Oh my God, I thought, honking the horn and feeling embarrassed at having forgotten. Simultaneously I was amazed that in her current state she could remember our joyous tunnel ritual. Though her body was rapidly withering away, the youthful garden in her heart still bloomed. A few moments later, I glanced at her and she had again nodded out.

I pulled up at the curb in front of the emergency room entrance and ran inside. Grabbing a wheelchair from the front hall, I took it back to Naomi. She was weak, and her body felt heavy as I helped her into the chair. At the reception desk, I could feel my heart beating hard while I struggled to catch my breath. "My daughter is having difficulty breathing," I said to the receptionist. "She has cancer in her lungs." I hated hearing myself say these words in front of all the people in the room, *as if I were announcing a curse.*

A moment later we were ushered into a receiving room near the nurses' station. A nurse came in, and after I informed her of the situation she clamped a pulse oximeter onto Naomi's thumb, checked her pulse and blood oxygen level, and finally said, "Her heart is beating fast, and her oxygen level is way down." She then took a sterile package from a drawer, and opening it, she removed a plastic tube and inserted one end into a nozzle protruding from the wall. Turning the oxygen on, she adjusted the flow rate, then placed the breathing apparatus over Naomi's nostrils. Together we helped Naomi onto a bed, and soon after the nurse left, a doctor came in. He seemed about my age, late forties, with blondish brown hair and a mustache, dressed in a white hospital coat. After brief introductions, he sat facing Naomi and looked at her with a serious expression before saying, "I must ask you if you have a living will prepared." There was a stunned silence in the room as we tried to understand the question. Guessing that we did not, he added, "In the event that while we are giving you oxygen you go into a coma and become unable to answer questions, would you want to be placed on life support to keep you alive artificially?" Naomi could not reply, and neither could I.

"We need time," I said.

Then he explained that her blood oxygen level was about half that of a normal person. Because she was suffering respiratory failure, there was a chance that in getting oxygen, her diseased lungs would not be able to sufficiently expel carbon dioxide, which could then build to toxic levels in her body. "We are trying to bring her oxygen level up slowly, and we will take a blood sample and analyze it right now to see how she's doing," he said before leaving the room.

We sat silently a moment, then Naomi looked over at me and said plaintively, "Oh, Dad, there *must* be a cure out there somewhere!" Surprised at her earnest statement that showed she had every desire to live and keep fighting, I began searching my mind for something to tell her.

At that point, the nurse came back in to draw blood. When she left, I told Naomi that I had to call her grandfather and Jean. Then taking her cell phone from her sack, I headed for the door. "Maybe Grandpa could come up. And oh, Dad, can you get me some magazines from the waiting room before you go?" she asked, knowing that I would be stepping outside since the hospital did not allow use of cell phones in the building.

After retrieving a few magazines, I went out the emergency room door, sat on a bench, and called my parents. My mother answered, and in response to my update, said reassuringly, "I know it must be so difficult for you; Naomi is your daughter. But you are my son. Whatever we can do, please tell us."

When my father got on the phone, I asked him to come help us, relayed Naomi's request for him, and informed him of her consent to go back to Santa Fe. "That's good," he answered, relieved that the issue of going home had at last been resolved. "I will be there as soon as possible, no later than this evening." I gave him instructions from the airport to the house on Shotwell, then I thanked him.

I felt somewhat calmer by the time I called Jean and Sarah, who had just arrived home from the Albuquerque airport. Jean was astonished to hear Naomi had gone so far downhill since their morning departure. We promised to stay closely in touch as events unfolded. Next, I called Michelle in Florida to let her know we had to leave, and I found out that Tony was already in San Francisco on a brief business trip.

By now, Naomi's oxygen level was rising, and the blood test results were back, showing no toxic side effects. Also, she stopped passing out. "What do you think about the living will?" she asked when I appeared in her room.

"If it were me, I would not want to be hooked up to a machine keeping me alive," I answered.

"That's the way I feel, too," she said.

I told the doctor that chest X rays had been done recently but the films were in town at Andrei's. When he had tried to contact Dr. Muirhead, she could not be reached, so a lab technician wheeled a portable X-ray machine in and took an image of Naomi's lungs. The results showed considerable congestion from cancer, and something else, most likely pneumonia. As a result, a portable oxygen tank and supplies were ordered for us. While we sat together waiting, the delay seemed interminable. Finally, Dr. Muirhead visited us. Kneeling down, she put a hand on Naomi's leg and smiled gently into her face. Naomi still had a magazine on her lap, and pointed to a picture of a sandy beach and palm trees by a blue ocean. Looking up at the doctor, she said, "Wouldn't you just love to be there?" Dr. Muirhead's eyes reflected the sadness she felt. Standing up, she looked at me and said, "I have all the scans ready for you to take home. You will need a doctor in Santa Fe. Please consider hospice help." At last, the rental company arrived with the oxygen equipment, and we left the hospital.

It was dusk when we began driving back to Shotwell. Neither Naomi nor I was afraid, but simply taking one step at a time. I sensed that we had passed into a tunnel of sorts. The outside world was shrouded, *but we could see inside, and there was light at the end.* I felt boundless love for my dear daughter who, ten hours ago, had roused herself from unconsciousness just long enough to prompt me to honk the horn, reminding me to be joyful and remember happiness. She was now my queen and I longed to serve her—nothing else mattered.

NOT BURNED BY FIRE

I am proud of your strength, my dear body and soul.

My father had arrived at the house before us, and together, we planned the trip home. He had researched air ambulance services, and although they were very costly, he thought Naomi's condition warranted the expenditure. After much discussion, we booked reservations on an air ambulance for the sake of speed and comfort, not knowing how much longer Naomi had to live.

The next day, we prepared for our journey home. On his hands and knees amidst suitcases and boxes, my father neatly packed Naomi's belongings while she gave orders from her bed.

After dinner, Naomi asked to go for a short drive, saying, "I've been inside all day. I need to get out." My father was tired and declined to join us, so she pushed her walker out to the car while I followed alongside with the oxygen equipment. Having no particular destination in mind, we headed to Twin Peaks and drove through the neighborhoods looking at houses. It felt surreal: we were out for an enjoyable ride, but Naomi was next to me dying. Gazing out the window, she suddenly exclaimed, "Look at these houses, Dad. They have *lawns!*" Returning home, it took both my father and I to get her in the house with the oxygen equipment. Exhausted by the time she had reached her bed, she looked up at my father and said, "That was quite a day!"

The next morning, Wednesday, the ambulance showed up at 9:00 A.M. to take us to the airport. Tony, who had come to see us off, was no doubt shocked to find my father with us and Naomi connected to an oxygen tank. She looked up from the couch and said, "Sorry I didn't get to go sailing with you."

"Oh, that's okay. Another time!" he answered, smiling.

Three medics came in and began preparing us for the trip. Forms needed to be signed, and Naomi's condition carefully monitored. Her blood oxygen level was below normal, and her heart rate high. When it was time to get in the ambulance, Naomi glanced up at me with the oxygen equipment connected to her face and a look that said, "I don't like this!" She then asked for her walker and began stepping toward the street, stopping to rest every few feet. The medics had been prepared to wheel her out in a stretcher, but my father, knowing that Naomi abhorred being an invalid, took one of them aside and said, "Let her walk as far as she can."

As the medics lifted Naomi onto the stretcher and put her inside the ambulance, my father kissed her good-bye. It was difficult for him, realizing he probably would never see her again. Then saying good-bye to my father and Tony, I got into the ambulance with Naomi. Fifteen minutes later we were driving onto the runway beside a group of private jets. There the waiting air ambulance crew took Naomi into their care. A nurse received current stats and began monitoring her vital signs while she still lay on the stretcher. I noticed that she looked tired as the Learjet pilot and copilot carefully lifted her into the plane and set her gently in a seat. The pilot, a strong, trim fellow who looked as though he had served in the air force, told me that our Learjet would fly at 41,000 feet, higher than commercial jets, and faster.

Within minutes we had priority clearance for takeoff and were in the air. Naomi looked at me sitting next to her in the stuffy little seating area behind the open cockpit and said, "I was really embarrassed by the ambulance showing up at the house this morning! It wasn't necessary. It scared the neighbors!" Amazingly, Naomi still cared that neighbors whom she hardly knew might be offended by the emergency team arriving at the house.

The two pilots talked casually as they flew, and just behind them, the nurse and I talked. She offered me a beverage, but I declined, saying, "There's no bathroom in this plane!" Naomi dozed off, the steady hiss of the oxygen always present. Landing at the small airport in Santa Fe, our jet pitched around in strong crosswinds before touching down on the runway, where another ambulance with three medics awaited us. Once records were transferred, we were on our way home.

At the house, Jean and Sarah were waiting. Although Naomi had left for California only six months ago, we all felt as though she had been gone for ages, and now, after a long and difficult journey, body broken but spirit intact, she had arrived home. A sign that Jean and Sarah had made, saying, "Welcome Home, Naomi—We Love You," was waiting in her room. As the medics carefully brought her into the house, Sophie and Chaco charged up to the gurney and licked her face and hands.

The oxygen supplier had arrived with tanks and equipment and a hospice care nurse. A portable toilet and wheelchair were placed in Naomi's room. We were taught how to monitor her oxygen level and heart rate and to manage the oxygen equipment.

So as not to be swamped with phone calls, Naomi requested that no one be told she was home. She was weak from fighting for oxygen, her heart rate was rapid, and her left leg and hip were a swollen mass of fluid and cancer. Eating was tiring, even nauseating, and her pain was unrelenting.

By now I had finally resigned myself to the fact that Naomi was dying, so it surprised me when she called Andrei the next day to receive a treatment. "Naomi, do you still hope?" I asked silently, in amazement. She also continued drinking her Ensure formulas, and when dinner was brought to her, she finished it—after three hours of nibbling. Always an avid reader, she then began a novel Jean had given her.

Late Friday, when she had just finished her second long-distance treatment with Andrei, she phoned her friend Adella from her wheelchair. Speaking awkwardly, as she labored to breathe while the oxygen flowed into her nostrils, she said in a weak voice, "Hi, Adella, it's Naomi. I'm back home now . . . I'm fine. I have a little pneumonia in my lungs—it's just a minor setback. I want to see you!"

Because Adella was on her way out of town with her sister, she asked Naomi if she could come Monday. "Definitely," answered Naomi. "I can't do much; but even if we have a picnic in my room, we can do *something*."

"That's great. I'll see you Monday. Naomi, I love you," Adella said.

"I love you, too," Naomi told her.

Soon after our arrival, I called Ann Brode in Santa Barbara to tell her Naomi was home. "It's bad . . . I don't think she has much time left," I said.

"I want to see her before she goes," Ann replied. "Do we have a couple of weeks?"

"No, maybe only four or five days, I'm afraid," I told her.

Ann was shocked, and had to make a decision fast. "I will call you back soon, Steven."

Later that day Ann called and said that Ben Sr., Little Ben (her son from a former marriage), and Carrie would be in Santa Fe on Saturday. Ann would follow as soon as possible after visiting her sick sister in Denver. I phoned Kathleen and arranged to bring her to the house on Sunday, then I scheduled an appointment with Arden for Monday.

In our home, there was a feeling that we were once again all together but under dire circumstances. We encircled Naomi with love, making her comfortable, monitoring vital signs, assisting her efforts to move about, and watching videos together.

Late Saturday afternoon, the three Brodes arrived from California. It was good to see them, although Naomi was weak and distressed. They stayed a short while, visiting with her in her room, and then left with a promise to return the next day. Afterward, I went into Naomi's room, sat alone next to her bed, and took her hand. Her left leg was propped high on pillows, and she was leaning back against more pillows and blankets. Her puffy face seemed transfigured. Opening her eyes, she gazed at me, and I began to cry, exclaiming through my tears, "I am so proud of you! You have brought all of us honor by your example. How precious you are!" Then squeezing her hand, I said, "I love you so much."

She seemed surprised at my tears and waited until I was finished, then in a small breath said, "I love you, too—*times two!*"

Sunday morning when I went into her room, she was again sitting up, this time with a pen in her hand, feebly recording a dream. When I asked her to describe it, all she said was, "I was on a blissful cruise."

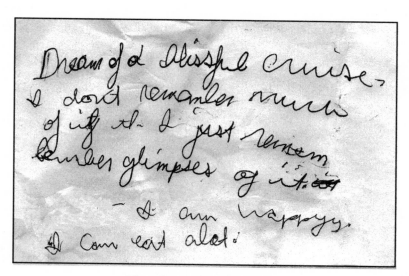

Naomi's recording of her dream

Later that morning, Preston Miller came to massage Naomi. On his way to our house, he had grappled with memories of the loss of his son Leander, but had overcome them by the time he knelt at Naomi's side and took her hand. Noticing how much she had deteriorated, as she sat in her wheelchair, pale and fragile, head occasionally dropping onto her chest, he was profoundly aware of being respectful, convinced that he had entered a sacred space. Moving around the wheelchair, he gently worked her neck, back, arms, and legs. All the while he could feel her letting go, allowing her body to soak up his touch as a sponge absorbs water. Naomi, mustering strength to speak, soon whispered, "You have no idea how good this feels." Drifting off, and coming to a few moments later, she asked, "How's Barbara?" And then, "How's the family?" As Preston continued working, it occurred to him that she might be feeling her form for the last time, and that they were somehow sharing it. When he had finished, Naomi said, "I love my body . . . it has been so good to me."

When Preston recounted these moments with Naomi, I knew immediately that *she had learned the code* and had at last become one with the ocean of eternal grace. Nothing could harm her now—not the shark of death, or the dark, or her aloneness in the rolling waves, for she knew she was embraced by God. I thought of the Atman, or eternal soul, and was reminded of a passage from the *Bhagavad-Gita* describing one who has reached eternal peace:

> *The bonds of his flesh are broken.*
> *He is lucky, and does not rejoice:*
> *He is unlucky, and does not weep.*
> *I call him illumined.*

> *Not wounded by weapons,*
> *Not burned by fire,*
> *Not dried by the wind,*
> *Not wetted by water:*
> *Such is the Atman,*

Not dried, not wetted,
Not burned, not wounded,
Innermost element,
Everywhere, always,
Being of beings,
Changeless, eternal,
Forever and ever. [1]

CANDLES IN THE NIGHT

*I understand God's love for me, and know that
I am going to be all right.*

On Sunday when I picked up Kathleen, I asked if she would like to stay at our house to be with Naomi in her final moments with us, and she agreed. Naomi had changed in the two weeks since Kathleen had been with us in San Francisco. At that time, they had talked about college and Naomi's plans for fall. Now, she was losing her ability to communicate, drifting in and out of consciousness. Walking into Naomi's room, Kathleen was startled and said to herself, "This is not my little girl anymore . . . she should have stayed in California. It's so disappointing for her." From that moment on, Kathleen barely left Naomi's side.

That evening the Brodes came to the house. Naomi was sitting up in bed, breathing strenuously with her chin on her chest, and her face was puffy. Beads of sweat covered her forehead. Her eyes were closed, and with each breath, her shoulders seemed to rise slightly and fall, as if trying to make more room in her lungs for air. She had complained of being hot, and we put a small portable fan on her dresser, directing a breeze toward her. A little group gathered by her bedside in silent support. Carrie seemed transfixed, almost unable to look away from Naomi. Unopened letters lay on the bed, and Little Ben, noticing them, asked if he could read Naomi's mail to her. Sitting by her side, he read softly, his deep voice rich with sympathy and love. As he was reading, I wondered, does she comprehend the words or is she simply being present with our souls in these last dying moments?

The Brodes left, and Sarah, Jean, Kathleen, and I gathered with Naomi, propping pillows all around her to help her sit up. I took her right hand while Sarah held her left, and then I spoke to her, with tears rolling down my cheeks. "Oh, Naomi! Remember our time in San Francisco? Our walks in the Golden Gate Park, driving across the bridge, and days at the ocean?" Sarah had begun crying, and I was choked up, but continued. "Remember the tea garden, Seal Rock Inn, and..." Suddenly Naomi's head came up, and lurching forward with eyes wide open, she blurted out, "Don't do this!" then fell back. Startled, I dropped her hand and retreated a bit in bewilderment. Her voice was so strong. What did she mean by *Don't do this?* What had happened? We had gathered near her in sympathy, held her hands, and cried. I was remembering good times we had experienced together in San Francisco. What had she objected to? Was it my sadness, my holding on to her? She always hated pity. Could she have been talking to herself, saying, don't die? Regaining my composure, I remarked, "I guess she told me!"

Jean laughed and said, "I guess she did!"

Eventually it sunk in that Naomi was shifting between worlds and I was keeping her back, somehow obstructing her passage into the next realm. She was near the end of the tunnel, and light was streaming into her soul. When I cried and held her hand, she was telling me, "Don't be weak at this glorious moment—be strong!"

Speaking of the end of the soul's journey on this earthly plane, Bahá'u'lláh Himself had written:

O Son of the Supreme!
I have made death a messenger of joy to thee. Wherefore dost thou grieve? I made the light to shed on thee its splendor. Why dost thou veil thyself therefrom?[1]

It had been I, not Naomi, who was veiled from death. I concluded that a powerful spirit in her had resuscitated the last of her strength in a short burst so she could command me to be attentive in these final important moments.

We put a futon on Naomi's floor for Kathleen to sleep on, and then we left the two alone for the evening. In the morning, the hospice nurse arrived, and then the doctor, a tall, slender, bearded young oncologist. Naomi was in bed, pillows propped behind her, breathing hard and sweating profusely. Turning her head when the doctor entered her room, she glanced up at him and with much effort gasped, "Hi, how are you?" The doctor smiled at her and checked her pulse. A moment later he gathered in the kitchen with the nurse, Jean, and I, and said, "There is nothing I can do. Her body is worn out from fatigue. The lungs just don't have room for air anymore." Then after expressing his sympathies, he left.

I took a walk with Kathleen, who said, "Steven, if she dies in two days, I will know my mother was calling her. My mother died July 7 from cancer. I feel just terrible." Looking at the ground, she added, "Naomi is my only child, my sweetheart."

When we returned, Naomi was perspiring and hot. As I lifted a glass of water to her lips, tilting it slightly, she hardly recognized what I was doing. Water dribbled into her mouth, but then drooled over her chin. "Oh, Naomi," I pleaded, "please try to drink. You're sweating so much!" I attempted once more to lift water to her lips, but without moving her head, she lifted her hand and pushed the cup away. Evidently she could not swallow since her body was making such an effort to breathe.

Soon the Brodes arrived, and Ann, carrying a big grocery bag of food, was the first in the door. Kissing and hugging us, she took the food into the kitchen and went into Naomi's room to have time alone with her. I juiced part of a watermelon they brought, hoping Naomi would take some. Before leaving, the nurse handed me several mouth swabs and said, "Wet these, and try swabbing her mouth if she can't swallow." Going back into her room and standing by her side, I dipped a swab into the watermelon juice, trying to coax Naomi to swallow. Her eyes were rolled up, and she was gasping for air in short bursts. Frustrated and realizing the uselessness of my effort, I quit.

After lunch, the house cleared except for Kathleen, who stayed with Naomi. The Brodes went into town, Jean took Sarah out for some fresh air, and I went to Arden's office for my 3:00 P.M. appointment. As I pulled my van up in front of Arden's, it seemed as if Naomi's spirit called me, but I could not be sure, and I went inside. Facing Arden, I felt as though all the emotion had been wrung out of me. "Naomi's dying, and I don't know how long she has left," I told him. Suddenly I felt anxious being away from her. Staring into Arden's eyes, I said, "What if she dies and I am not there?" As before, we talked about control issues and learning to let go. Then at the end of the session, we both stood up, and I asked, "Arden, can I use your phone to call home?"

"Of course," he said.

Standing by his desk, I dialed our number, and Ann answered. When I asked how were things going, she sounded anxious and said, "Here, I am going to let you talk to Jean."

There was a pause as Jean picked up the phone. She said sadly, "She has passed. I got home at three o'clock and she had gone. Kathleen was here."

Hanging up the phone, I turned to Arden in disbelief and exclaimed, "Naomi died!"

We both stood still, almost unable to move. Then Arden said, "Oh, Steven! I am so sorry!"

"Maybe she needed us to leave the house before she could go," I reasoned.

We embraced, and as I was leaving, Arden said, "I will always remember and cherish this moment."

When I returned home, Jean related more details about Naomi's death. While Jean had been out, she had called and asked Kathleen about Naomi. Kathleen had replied, "She's breathing very, very softly." Shortly thereafter Naomi died, and Kathleen went into a stupor brought about by shock. Half an hour later, Jean arrived home after leaving Sarah at a friend's house. She went into Naomi's room and immediately sensed something odd. The oxygen was running, but Naomi was still. Putting her hand to Naomi's mouth, she felt no breath; touching her chest, no pulse. Kathleen stared at the body without a word.

"I think she is dead," Jean said.

A few minutes later, Ann arrived. Grasping what had happened, she removed the oxygen equipment, closed Naomi's mouth, lowered her eyelids, and said, "The time has come for our sweet Naomi to move on."

As I drove home from Arden's, bewildered and numb, I thought, Lord! She died at age nineteen. Nineteen is the most sacred number to the Bahá'ís. It contains all of life, beginning with the primal number one and ending with nine, the highest whole numeral before returning to zero.

When I pulled into the driveway, the dogs did not come running to the car with their usual greeting. Entering the house, I hugged Jean and went into Naomi's room. It was odd to see her body lying motionless, as if a lovely bird had flown away, leaving only its cage behind. Her clothes were in the closet, books on the shelf, and her track and field metals still on the wall. Everything was in place, but my songbird was gone. Then gazing at her face, I knew a positive transformation had occurred in her passing. It seemed as if an ineffable joy had touched her soul, and that in departing she had kissed her mortal form good-bye with great tenderness. Not a hint of struggle or care was left on her face; in fact, at the corners of her eyes, there lingered traces of a smile. We had fought hard, but my little boxer had been struck a blow to which she could not respond. I was numb, used to her getting up from being knocked down time after time, but some part of me realized that at last she had peace.

Moments later, I learned from Kathleen that the final, barely audible words Naomi uttered were, "God, God, God."

Within a short while, people began arriving at the house to help us with the body. Jean had called Ruth Lathrop, who proved to be indispensable in our time of loss. Ruth, a warm, steady woman, had assisted others at the time of death. Now her calm, untrammeled nature provided us stability and strength. As I was sitting with Jean at the dining room table, Ruth came to my side and quietly asked if we would like to keep the body for a few days. This had been Jean's request. It is a practice advocated by Rudolf Steiner, originator of the Waldorf schools, to allow loved ones to accompany the soul as it separates from the body. I was confused about what to do next: what *would* we do with Naomi? Ruth said, "We can take care of her here at the house for three days if you would like." I agreed but expressed concern.

"We will put dry ice around her. She will be fine, I am sure," Ruth replied.

"Well, if you are confident. I just couldn't stand it if a bad smell arose," I said.

"Of course, I understand. We will take good care of her," Ruth assured me.

Then Jean, Kathleen, Sarah, and I went into Naomi's room to bathe her. Stripping off her T-shirt and shorts, we washed and put angelica oil on her body, and shampooed her hair. Sarah picked out a white blouse and skirt, which we dressed her in. Later, Jean blow-dried her hair, and Sarah helped brush out her silky auburn locks. When we were done, Ruth and Barbara came in and helped us change the sheets by rolling Naomi to one side, replacing the bottom sheet, and then rolling her back to do the other side. Next,

Ruth's husband, Fletcher, arrived with sheets of plastic and twenty pounds of dry ice to preserve Naomi's body. Plastic was laid under her; dry ice was placed below the fresh sheet, both around her body and beneath her neck like a pillow; and then a laced white linen sheet was spread over her. Her left hand was positioned on top, resting over her heart, while the right stayed by her side. In accordance with Bahá'í custom, a finger on her left hand now bore a gold ring with the inscription: "I came forth from God, and return unto Him, holding fast to His Name, the Merciful, the Compassionate." I noticed that her nails still were beautiful from the manicure in San Francisco that she had so joyfully experienced with Sarah just nine days before.

A group of us gathered by her bedside, gazing at her—Kathleen, the Brodes, Barbara and Preston, Saifi and Freshtah, Ruth and Fletcher, Sarah, Jean, and I. Each of us remembered aloud a special way in which Naomi had touched our lives, and then we sang together. As we left the room, other people filed in, including Adella, whom Naomi had asked to come for a picnic that day.

Over the course of the next few days, as other people came to pay respects to Naomi, our house was flooded with flowers and showered with tender love. Meals were taken care of, the phone answered, the house kept tidy, and great sympathy shown to Jean, Sarah, and I. Naomi's body was cared for with loving compassion, and the only scent in her room was the fragrance of flowers. Each day, people sat in silence near her, meditating, praying, and sometimes crying. In the evening, when everyone had gone, the candles continued burning and lasted all night long. Sometimes in the middle of the night we visited her. It was during one such visit that Jean, sitting alone next to Naomi in the still, predawn hours, found, with the help of the angels, the inspiration for a poem:

Blessed be the angels sing,
With joy they guide you in a ring,

Like a halo 'round your head,
Gently tuck you into bed.

To mighty realms your spirit flies,
Through puffy clouds and deep blue skies.
So sweet the peace within your heart—
With God's love your journey start.

WINGS OF SPIRIT

Hardship will make us stronger. I think that in every situation there is good in it.

For days after her passing, I often felt Naomi's presence in spirit, always joyful and encouraging, as if saying, "Dad, remember the love that surrounds all of life. It is always near." Certainly, her short struggle had been intense, like an incandescent meteor burning up in the atmosphere. During that time, she had learned the code, and now from the other side, communicated in the language of the angels—a parlance that transcends thought and touches hearts.

The day after she died, Jean and I went to a cemetery not far from our house, looking for a place to bury Naomi. Entering the graveyard for the first time, I was struck by a sudden sadness, knowing that this place sealing her away from us would be her final stop. Chris, the funeral home director, guided us over the grounds, explaining that the cemetery was close to 80 percent full and that even if an area was unmarked, it might be already sold. A small road passing through the graveyard divided it into two parts: one an open field with a scattering of trees, and the other a more expensive area with a pond and a greater profusion of trees. As Chris walked us by the pond, every so often we would stop and he would look at the book in his hands and say, "No, this place is taken." Soon we stopped at a spot under the spreading branches of a juniper tree. Kneeling, Chris looked up from his book and said, "This is available." Just a few feet away, two trees had grown out of the same place, reminding me of the recurring twos in Naomi's life—the oldest of two children, the two car accidents occurring almost together, the dream where she had been given the healing fruit twice, the battle with cancer and then its reoccurrence, the pair of trees at the top of our driveway, and especially her many one-to-one relationships. At that moment, I felt Naomi's warm and gentle presence at my side, telling me, "This is it. Bury my body here." It was as if a magnet in the earth pulled at my feet and legs, holding me there. Immediately I said, "We would like to purchase this spot."

Two years had passed since it was discovered Naomi had a cancer that was spreading from her hip into her lungs. At that time, her chances of surviving were slim. Yet, despite the aggressiveness of the cancer and its spread, she made a miraculous comeback. She had graduated from high school while undergoing harsh medical treatments, traveled from coast to coast, modeled fashions in New York City during the Make-A-Wish Foundation trip, and been accepted at a prestigious art college. These were but some of her miraculous accomplishments. I knew from the physicians that her type of extremely aggressive cancer could have killed her in a month, especially as it was so advanced when first discovered. I profoundly appreciated the valuable lessons she left with me. First among them, love—a love so pure it can banish death, since death hardly seemed to touch Naomi. I knew that while thinking of her, I would always remember the way she charged forward with eagerness, embracing life fully.

When we buried Naomi, only close family members were present for the ceremony. Two days later our loving friends, knowing how stunned and grief stricken we were, boundlessly supported us in putting together a memorial service at a beautiful sculpture garden on the grounds of a local art foundry. Astonishingly, just five days after Naomi died, three hundred people attended the service. Simultaneously in Santa Barbara, fifty people gathered for a memorial.

As the days stretched into months, I noticed with fondness the two pine trees at the entrance to our driveway, remembering how Naomi had planted the seedlings as a child, and how one had died just months before her. At that time, I had replaced it with another, about the same size. Now, as if to prove the joy of being transplanted into a fresh garden, the new tree began to sprout vibrant, green growth, and even appeared to be overreaching its more established partner on the other side of the driveway.

Of course, I wondered if Naomi could have been saved. As I think back to my reaction to further treatments in Dallas, and my confidence that she could have regained her health strictly through a careful diet of detoxifying and cleansing, I remain mystified at the faith I felt then. The B-12 shots, wheatgrass juice, Epsom salt baths, and laetrile all came from my meditation and intuition. So did going to Dallas in the first place and then wanting to quit treatments after the cancer was gone from Naomi's lungs and appeared to have been destroyed in her hip. In fact, when the cancer returned, it was not in the original pelvic location. Now I am resigned that I will know all the verities only after I die, when the secrets are revealed.

There is a final note to this story, which could only have been expressed by spirit. On the first anniversary of Naomi's passing, Jean and I held a small remembrance gathering at our house, inviting a few friends who had been close to her. We all felt her presence among us, laughing, strong, and ever hopeful. I opened the memorial by saying how thankful we were for having been touched by Naomi's brief yet inspirational life, and then Jean read a poem she had written. Finally Barbara Miller asked us to all join in worship, borrowing from an old American Indian tradition. Using supplies she had brought and others we collected outside, each person made little cloth bundles stuffed with herbs—lavender, sage, rose petals, and more—made holy by our prayers. Then we tied them all together, each one connected to the next, creating a long chain of prayer bags. By the time we had finished, it was early evening, and everyone walked outdoors to the grassy area by our blooming flower garden.

A light rain had fallen, and storm clouds were now gathering—an amazing sight after weeks of high-desert drought. Even more surprising, a clap of thunder sounded as we made a circle, and each of us held the string of bags we had knotted together. One by one, amidst our tears and a sprinkle of moisture, we revealed our prayers. Suddenly I realized, *but this is my dream, the one where people came together on the seashore, in remembrance of their dear friend who learned the code of the sea and, after speaking with the shark, vanished in the ocean. They placed little prayer offerings on a shelf, then tied them all together with a string . . . which is what we have just done!* And now, on the seashore I could see a heart traced in sand.

As we stood prayerfully together, the sky cleared slightly and a marvelous light that was imbued with otherworldly colors surrounded us. A rainbow suddenly emerged, and someone said, "Look up there!" At that moment two doves appeared above us, as if coming only for us, a little circle of people holding their string of prayers, and they began the most amazing display of flying I had ever seen. Over and over again they flew upward in a tight spiral, their wings almost touching, and then plunged steeply down before beginning their spiraling ascent again, all the while reflecting the last fading rays of golden sunlight on the undersides of their rapidly beating wings. They were sending Morse code-like signals to our astonished eyes: "This is joy! This is love! What bliss!" Enthralled by these wings of spirit, I reminded myself, "There is the pairing again. *It must be her!*" Many others in the circle gasped, or held their breath. Barbara was the first to speak, saying, "Thank you, Naomi!" Then one of the children crooned, "I hope she keeps sending us messages like that, showing us everything is okay!"

As indeed I am sure it is.

* NOTES

CHAPTER ONE
1. Bahá'u'lláh, *The Hidden Words of Bahá'u'lláh* (Wilmette, IL: Bahá'í Publishing Trust, 1975), p. 3.

CHAPTER THREE
1. Matthew 19:21
2. Bahá'u'lláh, *Gleanings from the Writings of Bahá'u'lláh* (Wilmette, IL: Bahá'í Publishing Trust, 1971), p. 328.

CHAPTER FIVE
1. `Abdúl-Bahá, *Selections from the Writings of `Abdúl-Bahá* (http://bahai.attach.net/index.html).
2. Bahá'u'lláh, *Prayers and Meditations* (Wilmette, IL: Bahá'í Publishing Trust, 1971), p. 219.

CHAPTER SEVEN
1. Cited in *Literature World Masterpieces* (Englewood Cliffs, NJ: Prentice-Hall, 1995), p. 176.

CHAPTER TWELVE
1. `Abdúl-Bahá, *Bahá'í Prayers* (Wilmette, IL: Bahá'í Publishing Trust, 1985), p 37.
2. Job 1:21.
3. Bahá'u'lláh, *The Hidden Words of Bahá'u'lláh* (Wilmette, IL: Bahá'í Publishing Trust, 1975), p 11.

CHAPTER THIRTEEN
1. *The Independant* (11 Feb 1999): 73.

CHAPTER FOURTEEN
1. Job 3:23-26.
2. Job 3:23-26.
3. Job 2:10.
4. Cited in *Fire & Gold* (Oxford, UK: George Ronald, 1997), p. 38.

CHAPTER FIFTEEN
1. John 1:1-5.
2. Bahá'u'lláh, *Gleanings from the Writings of Bahá'u'lláh* (Wilmette, IL: Bahá'í Publishing Trust, 1971), p. 326.

CHAPTER SEVENTEEN
1. Bahá'u'lláh, *Gleanings from the Writings of Bahá'u'lláh* (Wilmette, IL: Bahá'í Publishing Trust, 1971), p. 129.

CHAPTER EIGHTEEN
1. Bahá'u'lláh *The Hidden Words of Bahá'u'lláh* (Wilmette, IL: Bahá'í Publishing Trust, 1975), p. 19.

CHAPTER NINETEEN
1. Bahá'u'lláh, *Gleanings from the Writings of Bahá'u'lláh* (Wilmette, IL: Bahá'í Publishing Trust, 1971), p. 120.

CHAPTER TWENTY
1. Bahá'u'lláh, *Bahá'í Prayers* (Wilmette, IL: Bahá'í Publishing Trust, 1985), p. 87.
2. Bahá'u'lláh, *Bahá'í Prayers* (Wilmette, IL: Bahá'í Publishing Trust, 1985), p. 219.

CHAPTER TWENTY-ONE
1. Cited in *Literature World Masterpieces* (Englewood Cliffs, NJ: Prentice-Hall, 1995), p. 176.
2. Bahá'u'lláh *Gleanings from the Writings of Bahá'u'lláh* (Wilmette, IL: Bahá'í Publishing Trust, 1971), p. 296.

CHAPTER TWENTY-TWO
1. Bahá'u'lláh, *Bahá'í Prayers* (Wilmette, IL: Bahá'í Publishing Trust, 1985), p. 87.
2. Shu Ting, "Fairy Tales," in *A Splintered Mirror: Chinese Poetry from the Democracy Movement,* trans. by Donald Finkel (Farrar, Straus and Giroux, New York: 1991).

CHAPTER TWENTY-THREE
1.   Cited in *Literature World Masterpieces* (Englewood Cliffs, NJ: Prentice-Hall, 1995), p. 177.

CHAPTER TWENTY-FOUR
1.   Bahá'u'lláh, *The Hidden Words of Bahá'u'lláh* (Wilmette, IL: Bahá'í Publishing Trust, 1975), p. 11.

photo by Jill Martin

Steven Boone was born in Chicago, Illinois, in 1952. Raised in Illinois, New York, and then Washington, DC, he excelled in art at an early age, and in 1976 earned a degree in painting from the Maryland Institute, College of Art, in Baltimore, Maryland.

After graduating, Steven settled in Santa Fe, New Mexico, where he now resides with his wife and youngest daughter. His art studio abounds with landscape, figurative, and abstract paintings, some of which were inspired by the death of his oldest daughter, Naomi, in the summer of 1999. Exhibited in Santa Fe and on the Web, at www.stevenboone.com, his oil-on-canvas works resonate with the play of shadow and light.